From the Krays to Drug Busts in the Caribbean

To my family, Beth, Mandy, Ross,
Katharina, Ellie and Joe for
making me, me.

From the Krays to Drug Busts in the Caribbean

A Thirty-Year Journey

Ian Brown

PEN & SWORD
TRUE CRIME

ISBN 978 1 52670 750 5

A CIP catalogue record for this book is available from the British Library.

Typeset in Ehrhardt by
Mac Style Ltd, Bridlington, East Yorkshire.
Printed and bound in the UK by CPI Group (UK) Ltd,
Croydon CR0 4YY.

Pen & Sword Books Limited incorporates the imprints of Atlas, Archaeology, Aviation, Discovery, Family History, Fiction, History, Maritime, Military, Military Classics, Politics, Select, Transport, True Crime, Air World, Frontline Publishing, Leo Cooper, Remember When, Seaforth Publishing, The Praetorian Press, Wharncliffe Local History, Wharncliffe Transport, Wharncliffe True Crime and White Owl.

For a complete list of Pen & Sword titles please contact:
PEN & SWORD BOOKS LIMITED
47 Church Street, Barnsley, South Yorkshire S70 2AS, England.
E-mail: enquiries@pen-and-sword.co.uk
Website: www.pen-and-sword.co.uk

Contents

I'm standing in the middle of a dusty Caribbean car park in the blazing sun looking down the barrel of a gun. The man pointing it at me is sitting in a lorry containing fifty million dollars' worth of cocaine. It was time to run, and run I did as fast as my ageing legs would carry me before throwing myself into a ditch of stinking water. I lay there for a few moments trying to catch my breath then, coughing and spluttering, I sat up and wondered – how the hell did it come to this? I think it's time to go home!

Chapter 1

The Day the Roof Fell In

I suppose it all started with an early-morning drive from Keswick to Cockermouth with no cars on the road and scenery that just doesn't get much more beautiful. The sun was just beginning its 3000-foot climb before clearing the summit of Skiddaw, one of the highest points in the Lake District and the panoramic backdrop to the town of Keswick. Darkness had started to fade and the sky showed the first signs of a wonderful pink, clear light. The country road twisted and turned as it followed the shores of Bassenthwaite Lake. The water in the lake, still dark and imposing, would soon become a shimmering mirror reflecting the beauty of the countryside. It is a tourist's delight and a photographer's dream, but I am neither of these as this is my journey to a much darker place. I am on my way to punch the time clock for the 6.00 am shift before spending eight hours deep in the ground, best part of a mile under the sea, working on the coalface at St Helens Coal Mine in Siddick, Cumberland.

Siddick was not much more than a village with a general store, a butcher, a baker, but no candlestick maker. It had a couple of pubs and terraces of miners' cottages all sitting in the shadows of the towering pithead winding gear, which dominated the skyline for miles around.

The mine opened in 1880 and now, in the early 1960s, it was still producing and not yet aware of the impending demise of the coal industry. The whole village was reliant on the mine and local income fluctuated in tandem with the mine's prosperity. Its noise was the soundtrack to village life: the whirr of the pithead motors, the blast of the hooter signalling the start and end of each shift, the clatter from the railway as trains arrived to be loaded with the result of the men's labour and the rumble of the lorries, which trundled along the street filling the air with coal dust. But this din wasn't considered an inconvenience to the villagers. In fact, it was a comfort, as it assured them that all was well at the pit, and there would be money in their pockets and purses at the end of the week.

I was employed as a face electrician and on this particular day, halfway through a week of early shifts, everything pointed towards it being just another day at the coalface. The daily routine never varied. I would arrive at our pithead workshop minutes before 6.00 am, punch a time card into the clock and make a cup of tea, before my fellow tradesmen and I donned overalls and helmets, checked the helmet-light battery and set off down the shaft ready to walk almost a mile to the coalface. The walk was always accompanied with the usual banter about football, rugby league, women, sex and the number of pints consumed in the pub the night before. It was also essential to know who had the best sandwiches in their bate box for that day. The older miners reckoned they could tell how long you had been married by the contents of your box and the filling in your sandwich. Their theory was that newlyweds always had the best sandwiches as the wife was still trying to impress the husband. By the time you had been married a few years you were down to dripping on a Monday and homemade jam for the rest of the week. True love was a biscuit or a piece of homemade cake. These men were like fortune tellers reading tea leaves. One quick look in your sandwich box and they would be able to tell you the odds on you winning the football pools, the age, sex and IQ of your children (and if you didn't have any, when they would arrive), whether your wife was pre-menstrual, your sexual prowess and the chances of you getting divorced in the next six months.

As electricians, our main responsibility was to ensure that the machine that extracted the coal from the face (the cutter) continued to work without interruption. Keeping the machine running determined the productivity of the mine and consequently how much cash went in everyone's pocket at the end of the week. When the shift was over, it was back to the pithead for a quick shower and then over the road to the pub. Having realized that he couldn't pull pints fast enough to satisfy the thirst of throats dry with coal dust, the landlord of our local hostelry devised a way to ensure the glasses were always full. At the sound of the hooter signalling the end of the shift, he would start pulling beer into an old tin bath placed under the taps and, as the colliers came through the door, he would fill the beer tankards from the bath and line them up along the bar. No payment was asked for or given at this stage as that would be a waste of precious drinking time. A couple of pints later the men would leave their money on the counter, shout abusive farewells to their mates and head off home, where their wives would be expected to be ready with a bowl full of something hot.

On this particular day, the only deviation from the norm had come about twenty minutes before the end of the shift when the cutter broke down in the middle of a fault. A fault is a variation in the coal seam, which causes it to rise and fall, necessitating the cutter to cut through hard rock to keep the floor level. It also means that the roof becomes unstable with heavier rock hanging on to the coal. This situation is one of the biggest dangers in coal mining as the heavier rock can break away and crash to the ground, creating a cave with an unstable roof. So, there we were, trying to drag the cutter out of the fault to work on it in safer conditions and ensure it was working again for the afternoon shift. We always worked in pairs, but after about fifteen minutes John, who was working with me that day, said, 'We have got to go. I've just remembered my wife has a dentist appointment at three and I have to look after the kids.' So we got up off our hands and knees and set off back to the pithead. After a quick shower and a quick apology to the afternoon shift, we left. Just another day at work.

I didn't realize when I arrived at work the following morning that this was the day that would change my life forever and send me on a journey that would have been unimaginable even in my wildest dreams. The workshop was unusually loud with a buzz of continual chatter. Something must have happened. It wasn't long before I found out that yesterday, at the end of our shift, and before the afternoon shift got to the face, the roof had fallen in, burying the cutter under thirty-plus feet of assorted stone and debris. Glancing up, I saw John looking at me. Words weren't necessary. We knew that if it wasn't for his wife's dental appointment, we would have both been buried under a pile of rock.

Over the next few days I started to reassess my life. I had only taken the job because there was nothing else available, and I needed to provide for my wife and new baby. There was no history of coal mining in my family, I was a pampered southern boy and the job terrified me every day. You never knew when the explosive sound of the roof falling and settling onto the pit props would erupt in your ears. It could be once or twice a day. When that noise reverberated through the pit and a cloud of coal dust blew causing total blackness, you realized you'd been crawling on your hands and knees, and were hanging on to a pit prop sweating and shaking with pure fear. It wasn't the best way to spend your working day.

A few years later in 1967, Martha and the Vandellas released a song, *Nowhere To Run*, with the lyrics, 'Nowhere to run to baby, nowhere to hide.' Every time I heard that song come on the radio I was back down the mine in the pitch black, scrambling about on my hands and knees. For some reason it was never one of my favourite records.

I needed something new, but I lacked qualifications. I tell a lie. I had a piece of paper which told anyone who might be interested that I was a qualified electrical torpedo fitter, but there just weren't many torpedoes left in the Lake District or anywhere else for that matter. But before we get on to this, if I'm going to tell my story properly, I need to go back to the beginning and tell you something of my upbringing, which was just about as normal as any childhood of that time could be.

Chapter 2

All At Sea

I am pre-war by exactly a year, being born in September 1938. My family history is not rich with adventure or epic travel and has always been linked to the Medway towns. These are the south-east England areas of Gillingham, Chatham and Rochester, which straddle the river Medway. There is a family myth that somewhere down the line a great aunt many times removed had once been courted by Mungo Park, the Scottish explorer who died in 1806 on his second failed attempt to find the source of Africa's Niger River. What he was doing in the Medway towns, however, could never be established.

My father's family were Chatham Dockyard tradesman dating back generations. At the outbreak of the Second World War, many of these highly-skilled men were given reserved occupation status in order that they could continue preparing the warships so desperately needed to combat the German fleet.

By 1940 Chatham was being bombed constantly and my father decided to move his family – my mother, my older brother and sister, who were twins, and me – to a safer place. He rented a rambling old farmhouse at Stockbury, a village some fourteen miles from Gillingham. I have only fleeting memories of the war years, which include Mickey Mouse gas masks, doodlebugs, and picking up tinfoil dropped by bombers using it to interfere with something called radar.

We returned to our Gillingham home when I was eight, a larger family, thanks to the arrival of my younger brother who was conceived during the victory celebrations. There is nothing much to say about my academic achievements. I failed the selection board for the eleven-plus. At the interview, I was asked the meaning of the wording in the hymn, which states 'there is a green hill far away, without a city wall'. When I said it meant it didn't have a city wall, the look on their faces told me my days of academia were over before they started. I did manage to pass the thirteen–plus and attend a technical school in Chatham, but my only real interests there were football and tennis.

Like most local teenagers at the time, I sat the entrance exam for an apprenticeship in Chatham Dockyard. Trades were offered to boys in the order they'd finished in the exam, with the most sought-after going to the highest achievers. By the time it came to me, the only trade left was as an electrical torpedo fitter, which just happened to be the same trade my brother had taken five years earlier. Seeing this as an omen, I accepted.

The five-year apprenticeship passed with few highlights. However, outside of work, I qualified for Junior Wimbledon (although, of course, in those days Junior Wimbledon was no more than the British Junior Championships, which happened to be played at Wimbledon). I was seventeen at the time and took a week's holiday to play. I won two rounds and, out of the sixty-four entries, I was the only one who was actually working. Tennis was even more of an elitist sport than it is today. I was also approached by Chatham Town Football Club to play in the now-defunct Kent League. By then my apprenticeship was bringing me £2 a week and, much to my delight, at the end of each football match I found 30 shillings tucked into my boot. I was the envy of most of my mates, as to them I had almost certainly reached millionaire status.

The event that was to change the direction of my life was playing in a mixed-doubles badminton match opposite serving Marines and Wrens. My ability to play was greatly diminished as my focus on the shuttlecock was consistently distracted by the beauty of a young Wren on the other side of the net. I have no idea what the result of that match was, but I know I won something wonderful that night, the heart and later the hand of my wonderful wife, Beth.

Our romance was made more difficult when the Royal Navy decided to transfer my new love to the recruitment office in Newcastle. It didn't take long for us to decide that a weekend together once a month was never going to be enough. Although she managed to secure a transfer back to the Ministry of Defence in London, we decided to get married when I finished my apprenticeship.

National Service was still in existence, but that was not a problem as I was in the last year of studying for a Higher National Certificate in Electrical Engineering and a deferment was guaranteed. It had already been announced that conscription would end in 1961 and my deferment would take me past that date.

In October 1959, we married in St John's Church in Beth's hometown of Keswick. The honeymoon in Scotland was only a few days as I had to be back to play football the following Saturday. We rented a flat and she started working as a civilian secretary for the Marines. Meanwhile, I was working in the dockyard as a fully-fledged electrical torpedo fitter on the princely wage of £10 and one shilling a week. With Beth's wages and the extra from football, we had managed to earn what was, in those days, everyone's ambition: £20 a week, £1,000 per year. All was well with the world.

However, a couple of months into married life, our world was turned upside down. A letter in the proverbial brown envelope arrived from the Ministry of Defence. No alarm bells rang as I was sure it was just notification of my deferment. I only needed to be deferred for a couple of years to miss the conscription deadline of January 1961. To my horror, the letter stated the exact opposite. My deferment had been denied, my call-up papers were enclosed and I was to report for my medical the following Monday.

I duly attended and, when the time came to drop my trousers and cough, I tried to cough very gently in the vain hope that a certain part of my anatomy would fail to function properly, but it was to no avail and a large 'A1' was stamped on my paperwork. You will soon be on the parade ground enjoying your weeks of square bashing, I was told. Followed by two years of wages of twenty-eight shillings a week, of which eighteen shillings would go to my wife.

The next day at work we found out that four of us at the same stage of study had applied for deferment; two were married, two were single and one of each had been granted, one of each refused. That was the moment I discovered you must never use logic when trying to fathom the decisions made by civil servants in governmental departments.

As we sat, discussing our options and our chances of appealing, we tried to read the paperwork we'd been given, which seemed to be filled with nothing but wherebys, wherefores, forthwiths, notwithstandings, foregoings and hereafters. But there, hidden away in an obscure corner on a page near the back, was a paragraph which stated that as an alternative to National Service you could join the Merchant Navy for a period of no less than six years or until you were twenty-six. Should you come out before reaching that age you would still have to do your National Service. We hadn't come across a 'what if', such as what if we joined the Merchant Navy and in two years' time conscription was to end? We could hardly be called up for something that was non-existent could we? After mulling it over with our families, the two of us that had been called up decided to take a chance.

Three days after our medical we jumped on a train and headed for London. At that time, all the major shipping lines – P&O, Cunard and Royal Mail Shipping – were based in Leadenhall Street. Royal Mail was the first I came across and I went inside. After a short wait, I was ushered into the recruitment office where, much to my amazement, after examination of my newly-acquired certificate as a fully-fledged electrician, I was offered a position as a third electrical engineer in the Merchant Navy.

I was told to report to Royal Mail Lines' office in London Docks at 9.00 am the following Monday, where I would be 'working by'. Having no idea what that phrase meant, and filled with trepidation, I headed home to break the news to my wife, who asked a number of questions for which I had no answers. What I did know was that I would not be home when the papers telling me where to report for military service landed on the doormat and that I was to be earning 50 per cent more money than I was on now. The basic wage was £15 per week, with the chance of earning more than £20 a week while at sea. That was £1,000 a year without my wife's salary and the extra from football.

Beth and I talked long into the night about the best way to proceed, and decided that she would go and live with her parents, and find a job in the Keswick area of the Lake District. The following morning, I set off for London with a suitcase in one hand and a toolbox in the other, and arrived at Royal Mail's London dock office. I found out that 'working by' meant working on one of the ships while the electrical officer was on leave. I was given the name of a tailor where I could go and get measured for a uniform. The office manager told me that if I was sensible, I should be able to find a very good second-hand uniform. I was given a company clothing chit, which would cover the expense. The cost of my uniform would be deducted over a three-month period from my wages.

My ship was HMV *Durango*, a refrigerated cargo ship shortly sailing to La Plata, Buenos Aires, in Argentina. There it would collect a cargo of Argentinian beef and return to London about eight weeks later. On the Friday, I was called into the office and told the second electrical engineer officer had called in sick, and I was to take his place and to report back on Monday morning. This promotion carried an extra £5 a week.

The only water I had ever sailed on was a boating lake at The Strand in Gillingham and that was a self-propelled paddleboat, which you messed about in until the man on the shore shouted, 'Come in Number Seven!' Now I was preparing to sail the high seas on a 10,000–tonne vessel with no knowledge of what I was supposed to do or how to do it. I spent a tearful weekend with my wife before reporting for duty at 9.00 am on Monday.

It didn't take the chief electrical engineer long to conclude that the little I did know about marine vessels was confined to submarines, and all he hoped was that my limited knowledge didn't end with his ship being submerged. His instructions to me were simply, 'Mouth shut, eyes open, follow me, watch and learn.' He explained that in about four hours we would be full steam ahead and then I could make myself useful. 'Doing what?' I asked. 'Making a cup of tea,' was the reply. My life on the high seas had begun.

I had never been abroad before. The furthest I'd ventured from home was to Scotland for our four-day honeymoon and now I was bound for places I had only read about: Las Palmas, Santos, Montevideo, Rio de Janeiro and Buenos Aires.

My days at sea involved crawling around the refrigeration tunnels of the ship as I serviced the electric motors. One day, my chief electrician showed me his method of testing the electrical sockets in the holds. Wetting his first two fingers on his tongue he proceeded to stick them into the socket, placing them across the two pins and declaring them live or dead. 'You try,' he said with a grin. Like a fool I did as I was told, and was rewarded with an electric shock that threw me across the deck and left me lying in a heap against the bulkhead, much to the amusement of those nearby.

The next two years were largely uneventful. I wrote letters to my wife, read a dog-eared copy of *Lady Chatterley's Lover* (which was banned in the UK), watched cargo being loaded and unloaded in various South American ports, loaded prime Argentinian beef, sailed homeland and hitchhiked to visit my wife in the Lake District. In January 1961 National Service ended. It was time to start our married life all over again.

We found a flat in Carlisle and I got a job as a service engineer for Hoover, and started playing football for Carlisle United. Despite my enforced break, I still held the stupid belief that I could become a professional footballer. After a few months, I was offered the chance to sign as a part-time professional for the magnificent sum of £7 a week. Not wishing to lose my amateur status without some security, I refused and was quickly shown the door. My long and winding road to glory had turned into a cul-de-sac. Our first child, Mandy, arrived in December 1961 and I started playing amateur football for Penrith. Everything was going well until, as a result of my inability to sell enough washing machines and cleaners, Hoover dispensed with my services. That was when I took the job in the coal mine at Siddick.

Chapter 3

The Beginning of my Police Career

It was one of my wife's uncles who suggested that being over 5ft 8in and of average intelligence, I might just be capable of passing the entrance exam to the police force, something I had never contemplated before that day. Much to my amazement, he was right. My future was established. On 8 February 1963, the day before my wife's birthday, I set off to Bruche Police Training Centre, near Warrington, for three months. On successfully completing the course, I was posted to Penrith as a fully-fledged police officer. My probationary period lasted two years, during which time I was able to continue playing football for Penrith and Crook Town. I found police life mundane and longed for a little excitement. There are only so many sheep dippings you can attend without counting the sheep and going to sleep. At that time, there were many police officers with twenty-five years' service who had passed exams to become sergeants and inspectors, and yet they were still pounding the beat with little or no chance of being promoted. It was very much a question of dead men's shoes and nobody was dying.

It was my talent as a tennis player that came to my rescue. I won the annual Police Tennis Championship for the north west of England and this qualified me to play in the National Police Championships, which that year were being played in London. Sitting in the bath with my opponent after our match, conversation got round to the advantages of being in the Metropolitan Police as opposed to a provincial force. I discovered, that at the age of twenty-six, he had already been promoted twice and was now a station sergeant, an achievement that would not be believed in the hills and the valleys of Cumberland. My wage at that time was £48 per calendar month, with no chance of earning more, as overtime was not payable in cash. I was shocked to learn that a constable with my service in London was taking home more than £70 per month. Furthermore, if you played football or tennis for the Met, the match was considered duty time.

Within days my application to transfer to the Metropolitan Police was winging its way to London. It had been an easy decision to make, especially as we now had two young children (our son Ross had been born in 1964). Much to my surprise, I was accepted and within weeks I was on a train to the big city. A couple of weeks training at Peel House was followed by my first posting to Croydon as a London bobby.

It didn't take long to settle into the daily routine of shift work and relax into London living. In summer, I played tennis every Sunday and I even managed to study enough to take the sergeants' exam. I was delighted to pass, even though it was almost certainly in the last place. The rules were that those who achieved the top 100 places in the exam were awarded automatic promotion the following year. The rest would have to wait for ten years in the hope of landing one of the 10 per cent of vacancies put aside for the near failures.

Once more a chance meeting in the most unusual of places provided me with yet another fork in the road of life. I was standing doing what one does best in the police station toilet when the detective chief superintendent walked in and stood beside me. I would not have dared to speak to him under normal circumstances, let alone here. So I was surprised when he turned to me and said, 'You've had a couple of good arrests lately. Ever thought about coming out aiding?' Aide to the Criminal Investigation Department (CID) was the first step on the journey to becoming a detective. Once accepted as an aide, you would spend the next couple of years in plain clothes, pounding the streets in crime hotspots or carrying out house-to-house enquiries on murders and other serious crimes. It was your apprenticeship and hopefully, at some point along the way, you would be put forward to try and impress a three-man selection board of senior officers to recommend your promotion to detective constable. Standing, washing our hands in adjacent washbasins,

I told the chief superintendent that I had only just passed the sergeants' exam as a qualifier and hadn't considered what to do next. He looked at me and said, 'Don't consider, just get your application in now. Aides don't have time to study. None of them have passed the sergeants' exam, which would put you in pole position to get made up fairly quickly. Off you go son. I expect your application on my desk first thing tomorrow morning.' Thanking him, I walked straight into the police station and, with one finger, typed out my application.

Arriving at work for night duty, filled with romantic notions of becoming the next Sherlock Holmes, I was posted to a walking beat in West Croydon with specific instructions to be in the proximity of the local dance hall, *The Croydon Suite*, at closing time, where I was to act as peacekeeper. I did so and placed myself comfortably in a shop doorway, and lit a cigarette. My training had programmed me to stay there and observe. Should a fight take place, I was to stay out of sight until it became necessary to pick up the pieces and either send them home or to the local hospital, whichever was more appropriate.

As revellers poured out the door, a scuffle broke out between three men, which rapidly escalated into a full-blown fight. It soon became violent and blood started to flow. To this day I do not understand why I decided to step into the middle of this affray and attempt to carry out my peacekeeping duties that way, but foolishly I did. To drunken youths, the sight of a police officer prompts one of two reactions. Either they realize the folly of their ways, say 'sorry officer', shake hands with each other and wend their way home, or they stop fighting each other and turn their attention to the police. Needless to say I got number two and, thanks to my own stupidity, I found myself in the middle of a fight that I wasn't going to win. After a few minutes I was on the ground and the men, having got bored of playing football with my helmet, decided to play football with me. The beating seemed to continue for an eternity as I concentrated on which shoe would land where.

Then I heard a squeal of tyres, the kicking stopped and a voice said in my ear, 'Here's your helmet, the van is on its way. Good luck.' As

I picked my sorry self up, I turned to see my three assailants standing quite still, heads bowed, with their hands cuffed behind their backs. A couple of seconds later there was another squeal of tyres as more help arrived. The men were bundled into the back of the van and together we went to Croydon Police Station, where I stood my aggressors in front of the desk sergeant. I explained the circumstances of the arrests, searched the men and placed them in a cell. The sergeant was impressed with my ability to single-handedly deal with three violent men and, as a show of his admiration, offered to buy me a cup of tea. As we walked into the canteen, we were confronted by three smiling gentleman in plain clothes who were waiting for their handcuffs back. Getting up to leave, one of them said, 'Next time you want help from the Sweeney [Sweeney Todd: the Flying Squad] it's easier just to pick up the phone.' They had just been passing and, seeing me in trouble, had dealt with the situation. In that moment my ambition to become the next Sherlock Holmes died and I just hoped that sometime in the future I could get myself on the Sweeney.

Chapter 4

The Hither Green Rail Disaster

With only a couple of weeks to go before joining the CID, my last uniform tour of duty was as observer on ZULU 1, the first response car in the Croydon area. It was the late turn on 5 November 1967 and the evening was passing uneventfully when, at 9.16 pm, a call came over the radio for any unit to go to Hither Green as quickly as possible, as a passenger train had been derailed. With blue lights flashing and our klaxon sounding, we got to the scene in seven minutes.

The site that confronted us in the darkness will stay with me for the rest of my life. A twelve-carriage express train travelling from Hastings to Charing Cross had crashed. Eleven of the coaches had derailed and four of them were on their sides. People were trapped, with some dead and others injured. Those who had managed to get out of the train were wandering about in a daze. Within minutes the fire brigade and ambulance service, police and doctors from the local hospital were on the scene, all professionals with a job to do. Among all the confusion and carnage was one other amazing sight; local people were converging at the side of the tracks armed with chairs and blankets, pillows, teapots and picnic hampers, filled with anything that might be useful. Somehow they set up a receiving station for the walking wounded and bewildered. We all went about the job of freeing the trapped and tending to the survivors.

Walking past one of the upturned carriages, I heard a voice call for help. I stopped and crawled underneath the train, and saw a man trapped half in and half out of the carriage. I called for assistance, and was handed a lamp to hold to provide light so a surgeon could amputate the man's legs there and then. To this day I don't know if he survived. Everybody that was there that night did an amazing job, but still forty-nine people died and seventy-eight were badly injured.

Chapter 5

Plain Clothes Calling

A fortnight later, my uniform was put away in a wardrobe where it would stay for the next twenty-six years. I was now in plain clothing.

The first few months as an aide consisted of day-to-day enquiries and I developed an insight into just how traumatic crime is for the victims. People tend to forget that for every criminal act there is a victim who needs support far more than the offender. Today's society seems focused on trying to find out why the criminal commits the crime rather than on supporting the victims.

On 9 May 1968 at about 6.00 am, six months into my new role, events took place all over London that were to change not only the face of the East End, but also the lives of police officers, criminals, politicians and people who had, over the years, witnessed gangland crime run unabated in the capital's streets, pubs and clubs.

Very early that morning Detective Superintendent Leonard Read, who was affectionately known as 'Nipper', had carried out dawn raids all over London. The targets were the notorious Kray twins and their gang. It had taken months of hard work to get to this point and Nipper was using a new method to combat major crime. Over some months he had persuaded witnesses who had previously refused to testify, as well as some of the Kray gang, who were becoming increasingly worried about the bizarre behaviour of 34-year-old Ron, to stand up in court and give evidence against them. He had promised them twenty-four-hour protection, a new life and a change of identity at the end of the trial.

Nipper had saved the arrest of Ronald Kray for himself. Expecting resistance from Ron, he had entered his bedroom with some trepidation.

He need not have worried as Ron, who was in bed with one of his young men, gave up without a struggle.

I was sitting in the canteen with my partner Don, pleased as punch to have just made an arrest, when in walked the detective inspector and asked what we were doing. We explained with some pride that we had actually arrested someone and were doing the paperwork. 'As soon as you've finished,' he said, 'go home, pack a suitcase, tell your wife you'll see her when you see her, go to the *King's Head* pub in Surbiton and there you'll meet a detective sergeant from Scotland Yard who will explain to you what's happening.'

Like a fool I requested a few more details, to which the reply was: 'If you needed to know I would have told you.' We finished our paperwork in double-quick time, and I rushed home and explained to Beth that I was going somewhere for some length of time and that I hoped to see her and the kids in the not-too-distant future. This was to be the first of many occasions when my wife had to accept a husband who walked out without being able to tell her where, why or for how long I would be away.

I drove back to Croydon, and then Don and I set off for Surbiton. We arrived at the pub, which was a quiet family hostelry, and walked into the bar. Unless they are trying to blend into the background, detectives are the easiest people to spot in a crowded place. They have a certain aura and command the space they occupy. We knew he was standing at the bar, so we went over to introduce ourselves.

Early that morning the Kray twins had been arrested together with a large number of their gang. At the same time, a number of witnesses had been removed from their homes and put under police protection. Our job would be to protect one of those witnesses twenty-four hours a day, working in pairs two men on, two men off. We could split the hours up anyway we wished, but at no time was the witness to be left alone. 'See the man sitting in the corner on his own?' asked the detective, indicating towards a small, skinny, bespectacled man nursing a half pint. 'He's your charge until the trials of the Krays are completed.' The detective added that he'd reserved us a room in a guesthouse across the road. One room, one bed, two chairs. He took us over and introduced us to 'Lennie the Book' and, with a nod and a wave, walked out.

And so began the most bizarre period of my life. In the hours that followed the Krays' arrest, each division of the Metropolitan Police was asked to provide two officers to be attached to the Kray inquiry. It became our job to observe, feed and entertain Lennie twenty-four hours a day, and try and keep some sense of normality in a situation that was anything but normal. But before I can tell you about my time with Lennie, it is necessary to explain the circumstances and events that led to his door.

Chapter 6

The Krays

There have been enough books written about the Kray twins to cause the axles of a mobile library to snap under their weight and I have no intention of adding to the list. However, I need to explain various episodes in the Krays' lives so you can understand the sequence of events.

Back in 1954, the Krays were gearing up for a violent clash with one of their rivals: the East End-based Watney Street Gang. With half a dozen of their best men armed with knives and coshes (thick, heavy sticks), they set off for *The Britannia* Public House in Stepney, the drinking hole of their intended opponents. However, the East End grapevine was on full alert and by the time the Krays arrived, the Watney Street Gang had disappeared into the night.

A young local lad called Terry Martin was finishing a game of poker when the twins arrived. Ron, who was becoming increasingly schizophrenic, was in full fighting mode and, seeing none of his enemies there, had to vent his frustration on someone. Dragging the young lad outside, Ron beat him as only he could, leaving him lying unconscious in the gutter. The fact that Terry hung on to life and pulled through almost certainly stopped the twins from swinging at the end of a rope, because at that time the death sentence was still punishment for murder.

Although a wall of silence surrounded the Krays, with victims and witnesses too scared to come forward, Terry would not be silenced for fear or favour. Once fully recovered, he stood at the Old Bailey and told his story. Although both twins stood trial, Ron took full responsibility and was sentenced to three years' imprisonment. Reg walked away unpunished.

Ron started his sentence in Wormwood Scrubs Prison and it was there that he met Frank Mitchell. Ron became totally besotted with Mitchell, although not in a sexual way, as Ron's preference was for teenage boys and certainly not for a man mountain of extraordinary strength who was strongly heterosexual. Mitchell had spent more time in than out of institutions since his teenage years and had been certified insane while confined in Broadmoor Hospital. It was from here that he escaped and broke into the home of an elderly couple, and held them hostage with an axe. He was known as 'The Mad Axeman' for the rest of his life.

Ron and Mitchell became firm friends and, on his release, Ron made sure that Mitchell received regular packages of goodies while inside. He also made sure that he had regular visitors, even when Mitchell was transferred to Dartmoor Prison, although Ron never visited himself.

Why, some years later in 1966, Ron set out to help Mitchell escape, will never be known. Perhaps it was the similarity of their history: both had been certified insane and Ron had escaped confinement to prove his sanity, and thought Mitchell, who had been detained indefinitely, could do the same. Maybe Ron saw it as a chance to prove that he ran London and that he could influence the Home Secretary into giving Mitchell a release date. Whatever the reason, Ron was certainly not capable of rational thought, for he was at the height of his paranoia.

On 12 December 1966, Mitchell stood at the side of Princetown Road, Dartmoor, and was picked up by two of the Kray gang, Albert Donoghue and Billy Exley. The escape took place without a hitch and, four hours later, Lennie the Book received a knock on the door. His nightmare had begun.

Opening the door that fateful evening, Lennie was confronted by three of the largest men he had ever seen. Exley and Donoghue were both well over 6 foot and close to 20 stone each. Between them stood Mitchell, a giant of a man whose physical presence made the other two seem small. Pushing past the diminutive Lennie, they walked into his flat and told him he was to keep Mitchell there until further notice. He was not to go to work or leave the house until Ron said he could. Lennie was petrified.

Lennie was the owner of a newspaper and bookstand outside Whitechapel Underground Station, which is how he earned his nickname, Lennie the Book. His main income came from what was under the counter, not what was displayed, as this was the birth of pornographic magazines and Lennie had a stash that suited every taste. Unfortunately for him, he had an ample supply of Ron's favourites and so Ron became one of Lennie's regular customers. No payment changed hands, as this was how business owners paid for the privilege of making a living in the land of the Krays. A couple of days earlier, Lennie had received a visit from Ron and the conversation was a little one sided with Lennie's only contribution being a trembling 'Yes sir' accompanied with a deferential touch of the forelock with his index finger to every question. 'You live alone don't you Lennie?' 'Nice little flat Lennie?' 'Spare bedroom Lennie?' Lennie confirmed all this was true. Ron carried on: 'Tomorrow evening you will have someone coming to stay with you for a few days. That will be nice for you won't it? We'd like him to be very happy. You can make sure of that can't you Lennie?'

At about 9.00 pm, Lennie responded to a loud knock on his front door and was confronted by two extremely large men who were dwarfed by the giant standing between them. Lennie landed himself a lodger. On that first night, he fed Mitchell with a fry-up from his grease-filled pan, gave him his bed, and then sat down in front of the television. At 10.00 pm, the BBC News hit the screen and Lennie sat bolt upright as the face of Frank Mitchell stared back at him. 'The Mad Axeman Frank Mitchell today escaped from Dartmoor Prison,' said the newsreader. 'A police spokesman said earlier that roadblocks are in place all around Dartmoor and we are confident there is no way Mitchell can escape from the area. The public should under no circumstances approach this very dangerous criminal, but if he is sighted they should ring 999 immediately.' Tears streamed down Lennie's cheeks as he repeated to himself over and over, 'he's in my bloody bedroom.' Luckily for Lennie, no one, including Mitchell, could hear him.

The next ten days were a nightmare for Lennie as the minders changed regularly and Mitchell became more frustrated by the hour. As Lennie sank deeper and deeper into a black hole, his only salvation was the arrival of Lisa, a lady of the night, who was to be Mitchell's companion right up until the end.

So here I was, crossing over to a guesthouse with Lennie looking furtively from one side of the street to another. We met the lady who ran the guesthouse and while we had no idea what she had been told about our reasons for staying, we decided that our first priority the next morning was to find out what our cover story was supposed to be. As soon as we got to the room, Lennie slumped into an armchair and lit himself a full-strength *Senior Service* cigarette, which he demolished in four or five pulls before lighting another from the butt's end. I realized that we were more likely to die from inhaling Lennie's smoke than at the hands of a criminal lurking in the shadows. Then, tears streaming down his face, he said, 'Can I have my sleeping pills? I need to get to sleep, and I can't sleep without them and a cup of tea.' What seemed to be a perfectly normal request was to turn into the bane of our lives and it soon became apparent that there had been a reason why the sergeant had given us Lennie's pills for safekeeping. Having taken his two pills, he would fight the effect and refuse to sleep. Drugged and dribbling, he would beg for more pills and, when refused, demand them angrily. Over the following months, this became a twice-daily ritual and our one attempt to wean him off, when we replaced his pills with Andrews Liver Salts for two weeks (his mood improved considerably until we told him what we'd done and then he flew into a violent rage) failed miserably. Lennie had been diagnosed as manic depressive years before and could only function, or so he thought, as long as he had his drugs.

The weeks passed by with trips to snooker halls, and dinners of jellied eels, pie and mash, pease pudding and faggots. Every other night (Don and I spent one night with Lennie and then one night at home while two other officers took over), I endured the discomfort of trying to sleep in a chair in a smoke-filled room as Lennie had the bed. One night, I had just managed to fall asleep when I felt a presence. Opening my eyes, I saw Lennie standing in front of me with his glasses askew in Eric Morecambe fashion. I almost laughed until I noticed he was holding a dinner knife. He looked at me with a glazed expression and said, 'I could have killed you if I'd wanted to.' This must have looked like a scene from a sitcom. Here I was, 6ft 2in and 12 stone, physically fit and still in my twenties. Lennie was 5ft 6in, weighed 9 stone wet through, was half comatose, drugged up to the eyeballs, 40-years-old, smoked at least sixty cigarettes a day and was threatening me with a knife that was just about capable of spreading butter. Of course, I did think it might have been different if he'd had a real knife. Lennie was an unstable character and thus needed to be treated with caution.

One day Lennie decided to punish us. He stood in front of us, and screamed that he could ruin our careers in a second by jumping out the window and killing himself. Don immediately left the room as we'd agreed that when Lennie started his ranting, it was easier to let one of us deal with it. We figured that we stood a better chance of calming him down one on one than two against one as it created less of a threat. So, fully in charge, I wandered across to the window, opened it wide and explained to Lennie that we didn't want to have to pay for any broken windowpanes. Snorting like a bull, he set off at full tilt for the window only to come to an abrupt halt at the window's edge. Turning to face me, and panting hard, he said he had reconsidered at the last moment and was prepared to give us one more chance to redeem ourselves. We were to treat him better and give him a sleeping pill. I left the room to make a cup of tea and found Don already doing it. 'Where did you go?' I asked. 'I went and stood under the window,' he replied. I asked if it was his intention to try and catch him if he jumped. 'Not bloody likely,' he said. 'If he came out of that window and didn't kill himself, I was going to jump on the little bugger's neck to make sure he succeeded.'

We had to get out of the guesthouse. We had to find somewhere with a bedroom for Lennie and one for us, preferably with a lock on the door. The sergeant in charge agreed so we rented a three-bedroom semi in

Sutton, south London, for six months. The trouble was we couldn't take occupancy for another two weeks. Suddenly, I had a wonderful idea. Lennie had never been on holiday in his life; he'd never left the East End, never seen rolling green hills, forests and lakes. Let's take him to Devon and show him where Mitchell was imprisoned in Dartmoor; take him to *The Elephant's Nest* pub in the village of Mary Tavy, where Mitchell used to drink while he was supposed to be on working parties (community jobs for prisoners who were nearing their release date). Let's relive all the stories Mitchell had told him back in Lennie's little flat. And so the four of us agreed to split into two and do one week each escorting Lennie round Devon. We thought we might even get him to dip his toes in the sea.

Phoning a relative who lived in Devon, I asked him to find us bed-and-breakfast accommodation on a farm in the middle of nowhere and then we set off for Lennie's adventure of a lifetime. He lay down on the back seat of the car with a blanket over his head to ensure he wouldn't be seen. Even though the Krays were in prison, Lennie was convinced they were capable of having him murdered.

Arriving at the farm, we were told that the single room was up the stairs on the left and the double to the right. We had only just opened our door when Lennie ran in screaming abuse about how we had done this 'on purpose'. We were then dragged to his room where he pointed to the window, which was protected on the outside with iron bars. Nothing we could say would convince Lennie that we hadn't secretly searched the whole of Devon to find a room with bars on it.

Over the next few days Lennie learnt the meaning of country life. He watched cows being milked, sheep being rounded up and he was even sent out to collect the eggs. Each evening, one of us stayed for dinner with Lennie while the other would drive to a local pub for an evening of peace and solitude.

I was enjoying my own company and a thick gammon steak one night when I was approached by the owner of the pub who told me there was a phone call for me. It had to be for me as I was the only non-local in the place. It was Don who said that Lennie had disappeared. I told him that it would be a crime to walk away from my gammon steak and as Lennie didn't have any money, and we were nearly two miles from the next farm and as Lennie had probably never walked two miles in his whole life, I would be back in an hour or so.

I was not in the best of moods when I arrived back and one glance at Don told me Lennie was still out there wandering the countryside. With no street names or bus stops, the chances of him finding his way back to the farm were low. So, armed with torches, we set off in search of Lennie, both holding a secret hope that he had been eaten by some mysterious Dartmoor yeti.

It is a known fact that in the open and in the dark you walk around in circles, so we reckoned Lennie should be on his fourth lap of the farm. No more than 300 yards down the lane we came across a small dry stone barn, one side of which was the lane wall. In through the gate we found the stable door and, pulling it open, found it full of hay. Shining the light of the torches around revealed nothing, but just as we were leaving we saw a slight movement of the hay. We directed our beams at the area, and suddenly the hay separated and a little head popped out. The glasses were bent and the hair matted with straw, but there was no mistaking the terrified face of poor Lennie. After we stopped laughing, we pulled the shaking Lennie out from the straw and asked him what the hell he was doing buried in a haystack.

It took a while for him to stutter out his explanation. Apparently, he had decided to be brave and go for a walk in the dark, but after 100 yards or so of complete silence he heard a rustling sound nearby. He picked up his pace, but the quicker he walked the more the sound seemed to follow him, and then there was a loud cough and then another. Lennie was convinced someone was after him; that the Krays had found out where he was and had arranged for him to be exterminated. Gathering every ounce of strength from his emaciated body, he had managed to run and when he came across this small barn he threw himself headlong in to the hay and burrowed down as deeply as he could.

We led Lennie back towards the farmhouse where hopefully there would be some food left for him. But before we could get there, there was another outbreak of coughing, this time from the nearby field. Lennie was ready to run for his life again, but, grabbing him by the arm, we led him to the gate to show him the herd of sheep blowing steam into the night air as they hacked and spluttered. Lennie had a lot to learn about country living.

On a far more serious note, this episode is a wonderful example of the myths that surrounded the Krays and illustrates the fear the Kray twins were capable of instilling in people who had the misfortune to fall into their path. At that moment in time the twins were most probably being put to bed behind their cell doors. They would certainly be on twenty-four-hour watch in a top security prison, and yet Lennie was convinced that this would not stop them from trailing him to the middle of Dartmoor and blowing his brains out.

After a couple more months of Lennie's tantrums and increasingly bizarre behaviour, it was time for me to move on to the protection of someone else, mainly to retain my sanity. Little did I realize that the next assignment would be just as challenging. One of the great things about being a police officer is that you never know who you will come across, although it isn't often that it is a scantily-dressed female whose purpose in life is to seduce every male who has reached puberty and has not yet succumbed to the comforts of the coffin.

Lisa Prescott was a lady of the night, a high-end escort who sold her wares in the clubs of London's upmarket West End. Among the clubs she frequented was *Churchill*'s in Bond Street, from which the Krays collected protection payments. One night, Lisa, a shapely blonde, a little on the plump side, was propping up the bar, drink in hand, scanning the floor for her next well-heeled client when she saw Reg Kray enter the bar with Tommy Cowley. Cowley had been recruited by Reg to help him find a young lady who would be capable of keeping Mitchell satisfied both physically and mentally. Much to Lisa's dismay, Reg's eyes fixed firmly on her.

Reg approached and told her that he had an Arab friend who needed a girl for the night, and asked if she liked Arabs. Lisa told him that she was not interested in the size of the man, but the size of his wallet. Clever remarks didn't impress the Krays, and without ceremony, a large hand grasped her arm and propelled her to the door where she was bundled into a waiting car. Refusing her request to collect her coat, Reg said her job was to take her clothes off not put them on.

Her heart thumped for the duration of the journey and when she arrived at Lennie's flat, she was told in no uncertain terms that she now worked for the Krays, and her job was to keep her eyes shut and her legs open. Lisa realized that she was in immense danger, especially as she recognized the towering figure of Mitchell from the picture that had been printed in the papers and broadcast on the news the last few days. Although Reg assumed that anyone who worked in a club he was protecting would do as they were told with no request for payment, in a moment of either madness or bravery, Lisa told him the only thing that got her knickers off was a handful of notes. Surprisingly, Reg left the flat to return half an hour later with £100. However, later on, Donoghue, who was guarding Mitchell, relieved Lisa of £20 for expenses.

Listening to Lisa tell her stories, with earthy humour and graphic language while sipping coffee at the kitchen table of a suburban semi in a leafy part of Surrey, became part of my daily routine. She would talk for a couple of hours at lunchtime – in other words shortly after she had got out of bed – and in nothing more than a negligee. One of the stranger parts of the tale was that Mitchell, who had a reputation for extreme violence, had fallen instantly in love with her and from that moment on had treated her as his princess.

Lisa was a self-confessed nymphomaniac whose sexual appetite could be equalled by very few men, except Mitchell. She said he had the physique of Adonis and the strength to go with it. His party trick was to pick up two large men by their belts and lift them until their heads touched the ceiling. She said he would make love for hours, get out of bed, do 100 press-ups and start all over again. In the darkness of that tatty spare bedroom in Lennie's flat, they were to share perhaps the happiest time of Mitchell's miserable life. He opened his heart to her and she became very fond of him.

He told her she was only his second sexual partner, the first being a teacher who taught in a school close to Dartmoor Prison, who he met during one of his unsupervised wanderings around the moor. They would have passionate trysts in the heathers with only the Dartmoor ponies for company. Mitchell told Lisa his version of the escape from prison. He said he'd been given a time to meet at a spot on Princetown Road and, not wanting to be recognized, he was wearing a mask he had made from his school mistress' knickers. How this escape ever took place is beyond comprehension as the thought of two of the Krays' henchmen, who were both pushing 20 stone, standing at the side of the road in the middle of Dartmoor trying to persuade a 6ft 4in giant to remove a pair of women's knickers from his head before bundling him into a car, is surely less believable than the most far-fetched farce.

Lisa stayed with Mitchell for his last five days on earth. She was his lover, comforter, friend and confessor. He was a simple man; a child's mind in a man's body, but that body bore the scars of the inhumanity of the prison system at that time. He had spent most of his adult life locked up, and his way of dealing with confinement was to rage and rebel. He would attack the warders at every given opportunity and would be rewarded with multiple beatings. On several occasions he'd received lashings from a cat-o'nine-tales. His only ambition in life was to walk down the road a free man. He talked of taking Lisa home to his mum. He said she would love her.

Teddy Smith, who was one of the Kray gang and considered himself to be something of a writer, composed letters begging for a release date for Mitchell, and Mitchell copied them with his spidery scrawl and sent them to *The Times*. They were published before being forwarded to Home Secretary Roy Jenkins, who ignored them. This depressed Mitchell who felt he had now swapped the relative freedom of his life in Dartmoor Prison for the confines of a pokey London flat. His biggest disappointment, however, was the fact Ron hadn't visited. He was continually asking when Ron was coming and the more he asked the more excuses he was given. The situation was hopeless and he could see no future beyond the walls of his new prison. The Krays were also in a dilemma as there were so few ways to deal with the situation. Even if Mitchell could be persuaded to give himself up, that would inevitably spell the end for the Krays.

But then Mitchell engineered his own fate. He sat down and laboured over a letter to Reg, in which he wrote that if Ron didn't visit him soon he would have to go and talk to their mother Violet. Whether or not that was meant as a threat, it is not known, but that's how it was interpreted by the twins and nobody threatened their mother. There was only one logical solution: Mitchell had to disappear for good. Decision made, the Krays turned to their old friend, south-east London criminal Freddie Foreman.

On the evening of 24 December 1966, ten days after his escape from Dartmoor, Donoghue came to the flat with the news that Mitchell would be spending Christmas at Ron's farm in Kent, along with his mother Violet. Mitchell was delighted, but his first thought was for Lisa and he asked if she could come along. Donoghue agreed, but said there was no room in the van right now so she could come along later. Turning to Lisa, Mitchell gave her what was to be their final kiss, told her he loved her and pressed a Christmas card into her hand. He and Donoghue walked to the waiting van, and the back doors were opened. Sitting inside were Foreman and Alfie Gerrard. Mitchell got in the back and, as soon as the vehicle started to move, Foreman and Gerrard produced handguns and opened fire. Mitchell died in a hail of bullets.

Returning to the flat, Donoghue found Lisa curled up on the sofa sobbing, with Mitchell's Christmas card open in front of her. 'I heard some bangs,' she said. 'They shot him didn't they?' She looked down at the card and read the words that had been so laboriously written by Mitchell: 'To Lisa, the only one I love, Frank.' Donoghue consoled her in the only way he could, by taking her to bed. She felt it probably saved her life as in the morning a mellowed Donoghue told her to make sure she kept her mouth shut and he pushed her out the front door. She didn't need to be told what a lucky escape she'd had. She just ran.

It would be ten years before Foreman admitted – on national television – to Mitchell's murder and revealed what happened to the body, which had never been found. In doing so, he caused the law on double jeopardy to be rewritten. Foreman had been tried for the murder of Mitchell, but had been found not guilty. He had, however, been convicted of accessory to murder and had been sentenced to ten years. When he told his story to the nation, he was fully aware that having been tried for murder once, the law stated that he could never be tried again. So he disclosed that the body had been taken to Newhaven, wrapped up in chicken wire, weighted down and dumped into the English Channel. Foreman's television appearance solved the decade-long mystery and also prompted the law to change although, moving at its usual snail's pace, it took years to do so.

Lisa's time under protection had been difficult from the start. At the beginning two male officers were employed to guard her, but this resulted in them being chased round the flat for days on end. They had both begged to be relieved and two women had replaced them, but Lisa fought with them constantly. It was decided that in order to satisfy her sexual needs, a man would have to be provided. Lisa suggested an old boyfriend who was brought in to keep her happy. Now that most of her waking hours were spent in the bedroom, it was only necessary to have one officer at a time on this detail.

Lisa would rise about midday, come down in her negligee and sit at the kitchen table with a cup of coffee, and, when she was in the mood, regale me with stories in graphic detail. She was a bubbly personality with an infectious humour, and she loved telling tales of the fantasies she had fulfilled for her clientele who came from every class of society and every level of wealth. She always said she should have been an actress, for she had played every part from Cleopatra to Marie Antoinette, Joan of Arc to Nell Gwyn and Catwoman to Tiger Lily, and had loved every moment. I often wondered what the value of her diary would be.

At about 2.00 pm, the boyfriend would appear and Lisa would hand him a shopping list. Then, while Lisa pampered herself, the two of us would go off to Tesco, him to shop and me to pay. Back at the house it was back to bed for a few hours before Lisa emerged again and cooked us dinner. We never ate together; mine would go on the table and theirs on a tray, which they carried back to the bedroom. The agreement for the evening was that I should leave them for a couple of hours and go and sit in the pub across the road. The signal that it was time to leave came from the repetitive banging of the headboard thudding into the lounge. Sometimes, just for the hell of it, I would wait until the rhythm of the headboard started to pick up its tempo before shouting that I was going out. It must have seemed strange that I should appear in the pub every second night and sit in the same seat, nursing a beer for a couple of hours while staring out the window, but the landlord never commented.

Months later, after the trials had finished and Lisa was free to go, I accompanied her to the offices of *The News of the World* as she picked up her fee for her blow-by-blow account of her time with Mitchell. She took it in cash in a plastic bag, gave me a kiss on the cheek and jumped into her newly-acquired VW campervan. A toot on the horn, a quick wave and Lisa drove off into the evening sun.

Over the next few months I spent time with several other witnesses, but only as relief cover if officers were sick or away. During my time with Lisa I had passed a selection board to become a full detective constable and was waiting for a posting. A few weeks later my orders were received and I was off to Peckham in south-east London.

The next two years were happy times, and I was learning from old detectives who knew everything and everyone in the area. They seemed to know who had done what before the crimes were reported. Their office was one of three or four local pubs and they achieved more with a pint in their hands than most of us youngsters did with hours of investigation. These were the days before 'isms'. We took the mickey out of each other and played practical jokes, without looking over our shoulder to see who was standing behind with a knife to stick in your back. We worked hard and played hard, and what happened at work stayed at work. It was a time when, apart from Brixton, the south-east of London was predominantly white. Immigration was on the rise and it became necessary for us to start learning the skills of dealing with people from different cultures. As time was to prove, we didn't do a very good job of it.

We never realize at the time how things learnt today might help later in your life. I certainly didn't imagine that the youths we were dealing with then would become the major criminals I would chase later in my career. One day, I saw a young man sitting on a wall watching us. He was known as a 'creeper', a thief who would wander through office blocks pinching anything he could. I went over and found a dictaphone on the ground behind him, and he was arrested and placed in a cell. But he wanted to barter for his freedom and we were only too pleased to trade in a dictaphone for the lorry load of shoes he led us to, which were being hidden underneath the railway arches in Rotherhithe. The arrest of two of his friends more than compensated for his release without charge. Years later he became a feared armed robber involved in the 1983 Brink's-Mat gold-bullion robbery at Heathrow Airport. He also had a reputation for being a man who would never grass!

Two years at Peckham flew by with every day being another step in my criminal education. As there were more vacancies for detective sergeants than constables who had passed the sergeants' exam, my promotion was almost guaranteed.

I passed the selection board for detective sergeant and waited with trepidation to see where I was to serve for the next part of my career. The posting arrived – detective sergeant at Branch C8. The Flying Squad! The Sweeney! My dreams had been realized. I could retire tomorrow and would feel as though I had made it.

Chapter 7

The Flying Squad

The Flying Squad became better known as the Sweeney, thanks to the 1970s television series of the same name in which John Thaw and Dennis Waterman played Detective Inspector Jack Regan and his partner Detective Sergeant George Carter. Yet the history of the squad goes back much further than that.

At the start of the twentieth century policing was very localized. Someone joining the Metropolitan Police would almost always spend the whole of their career at the same station. This worked very well as officers walked about among the local populace and came to know everything that was going on. They knew all the criminals as they'd watched them grow up from cradle to crime.

In 1919, following the end of the First World War, two factors would change this. The first was a marked increase in crime as the troops came home from the war to find there were very few jobs available. The second was the increasing popularity of the motor car. The last time criminals had been truly mobile was back in the days of Dick Turpin and London's highwaymen when their mode of transport was the horse. The car made it possible for burglars, in particular, to travel to wealthy suburbs of London where the pickings were much richer. Equally, the police, who had until this point travelled on horse or later by bicycle, could cover much more ground and had a better chance of catching offenders if they had four wheels at their disposal rather than two (or four hooves).

That same year, two decisions were made that changed the Met forever. Firstly, a number of stations were put under the same command and thus the Met was split into four areas. Secondly, something called 'the mobile police experiment' or 'scheme' was implemented on a twelve-month trial. The objective was to make officers mobile and to allow them to travel from one station's area to another in pursuit of criminals, without having to ask permission. There was, however, a small problem. The Metropolitan Police only had two cars, one for the commissioner and one for the receiver (the chief financial officer).

Two experienced detectives from each of the newly-established areas were selected to undertake the new experiment. It was time to find some vehicles, but, not wanting to waste money on an unproven idea, it was decided to present these officers with two horse-drawn wagons, which had been leased from the Great Western Railway. Making the most of the tools handed to them, the officers would hide in the back under the canvas hoods and spy through slits in the sides. They made considerable inroads into street crime and, after the trial ended, the experiment was considered a success and became permanent. Now was the time to invest in some motorized transport.

In July 1920, two well-used Crossley tenders were acquired from the Royal Flying Corps (which had merged into the Royal Air Force). With no front brakes and a supposed top speed of 40mph, they were capable of carrying a dozen men. They were fitted with aerials, which could be raised to receive messages in Morse code, but it was a receive-only system. If the officers need to speak to the yard they would have to stop at the nearest phone box.

One thing you can guarantee in the police force is that nothing is done in a hurry. It wasn't until there had been many instances when the tenders would drive up to a crime scene so slowly that the criminals were able to jump into their vehicle and, with a casual wave, drive away in the knowledge that the police didn't have the capability to give chase, that a decision was taken to purchase new vehicles.

There is no definitive answer to the question of where the name the Flying Squad came from, but the two most logical explanations are either because the first vehicles were previously owned by the Royal Flying Corps or because one of the first newspaper reports on the squad's activities in those early days had the headline: 'The officers swooped on the criminals like birds of prey.' There is no doubt, however, that the term 'the Sweeney' comes from Cockney rhyming slang: Flying Squad, Sweeney Todd.

The symbol for the Flying Squad ultimately became a swooping eagle with wings spread wide and talons curled, ready to claim its prey. This image was later to appear on the office stationery and on the badge of those who served. Special neck ties were designed for the male officers with silk scarves for the women and both were worn with pride by what was to become an exclusive band of officers.

Over the years, the squad continually reinvented itself as criminals became more sophisticated and better organized. By the 1960s, the squad was stationed on the fourth floor of New Scotland Yard in Victoria and was made up of eleven teams, each led by a detective inspector and a detective station sergeant. Each team consisted of ten handpicked officers, each of whom had established a reputation for being knowledgeable and capable of dealing with the highest echelons of the criminal fraternity.

There are many stories of heroic deeds and high-profile crimes being cleared up by the Squad over the years, but the 1960s was to produce one of the most iconic: the Great Train Robbery, which took place in the early hours of Thursday, 8 August 1963 at Sears Crossing in Buckinghamshire. Fifteen men under the command of Bruce Reynolds stopped the mail train from Glasgow by changing the signal from green to red with the aid of a glove to cover the green light, and a torch covered with coloured cellophane to create the red one. They seriously assaulted the train driver, Jack Mills, before escaping with 124 sacks of mail containing £2.6 million. The manhunt that followed immortalized the names of both criminals and police officers alike. The names of Detective Chief Superintendent Tommy Butler (the 'Grey Fox') who led the police inquiry, Jack Slipper, then a detective sergeant, and Bruce Reynolds, Buster Edwards and Ronnie Biggs became household names. Biggs' fame soared when he escaped from Wandsworth Prison and absconded, first to Australia and then to Brazil, where he remained for thirty-one years. Ill health and a desperate need for a British pint resulted in him coming back to England, only to find he had to serve the eight remaining years of his sentence.

When I arrived on the Flying Squad in late 1971, the most popular crimes were armed robbery and lorry thefts, and the importation and open use of cocaine was starting to raise its ugly head. Cocaine was expensive and while it had always been the drug of choice for the well heeled, its use had been pretty much kept behind closed doors. However, its prevalence among rock stars gave it a glamorous edge and, as always, the lure of big profit meant the criminal gangs were attracted to this world like moths to light.

I quickly settled into squad life. There were hard, long hours of often boring work, endlessly sitting and watching, hoping and praying that the information about a planned crime would materialize as you had been told. The information was not always from your own team and often you were asked to assist another team. Home life was a thing of the past as at the end of a long day the greater calling was for a few pints. Once the wife and kids were in bed, what was the point in rushing home anyway? It was easier to stay in the pub for a couple of hours and relax with people who needed relaxing as much as you did. It didn't take long to understand why, at that time, the squad had the distinction of having the highest divorce rate of any profession in the country.

Over the next couple of years, our squad of twelve men led by a detective inspector was to earn a reputation for recovering lorry loads of stolen goods. It all started with a phone call from a detective back in the CID office at Peckham, south London. He had received information that the driver of a lorry had been approached to have himself ambushed and his lorry full of groceries taken from him by a gang of thieves. The plan was for him to pull into a transport café where he would be kidnapped, put into a stolen van, tied up and driven to a remote place. There he would rest for a couple of hours, giving the thieves time to unload the lorry's cargo. Then, with great bravery, he would manage to untie his ropes and raise the alarm. Despite these heroic efforts, it would not be in time for the police to do anything other than recover the vehicle from where it had been abandoned, minus its load. The only problem was that the driver didn't want to do it, but had been intimidated by one of the gang and was too scared to refuse. It took a little friendly pressure for him to agree.

The following day, we occupied a number of vehicles in the car park of a roadside café, when, at the appointed time, the biggest articulated lorry I had ever seen trundled in. 'That's not a lorry, it's a bloody supermarket,' said my partner Dave, who was never short of a witty remark. As the driver came down from his cab, he was met by three instantly recognizable Peckham villains, who had jumped out of a nearby white van. A quick check on the van revealed that it had been stolen earlier that morning from a lorry park in Southwark. Whatever they did next, these three were already destined for a couple of year's holiday paid for by the good old taxpayer. After a couple of minutes, two of the men whisked the driver away in the van and the third jumped up into the lorry's cab. Our cars were started and the tail was ready to go.

The wonderful thing about chasing crime is that you never know what is going to happen next and you must be prepared to change your plan at a moment's notice. This was to be no exception as our adventure quickly descended into farce.

All we could see from the lorry's cab was the driver's head rising and falling as he bent down to examine something by his feet. This was followed by a loud grating noise coming from the gearbox. At one stage the lorry kangaroo jumped forward twice and then, after more grating and grinding, hopped backwards. Over the radio a voice said, 'Two forward, one back. Your throw. Two sixes will get you out of the car park.'

As we turned off our engines, we laughed as we realized the villain recruited to drive the lorry hadn't taken his HGV driver's refresher course and was completely unable to drive this brand-new state-of-the-art vehicle. Instantly the radio came to life from all our vehicles and typical ribald humour resonated from car to car. Most common was an officer offering to drive 'the bloody thing' for him. It was also suggested that we might witness and solve a murder in a few minutes' time because we knew full well that the leader of the gang, known as 'Jacko', who was renowned for his temper and violence, was not going to be happy that he had accepted someone's recommendation and employed a complete idiot as a driver.

It was time to lean back and relax with a vision of the white van sitting in a lay-by down the road expecting the lorry to drive past at any moment. Time also for one of the team to open the betting on how long it would be before the van came back. Everyone pledged £1 and chose their preferred time. The crazy part of this is that you didn't want to win the bet because when this is all over and you're down the pub, it will be you that buys the drinks with your winnings and there won't be enough to cover the bill.

Whoever had twenty-seven minutes was crowned victor as at that exact time the white van returned and skidded to a halt alongside the lorry. The incompetent driver was subjected to a tirade of foul abuse and a couple of minutes of Jacko's enormous finger trying to poke its way through his ribcage. Then the proper driver jumped up into the passenger seat and gave lessons to the village idiot. Ten minutes later we were on the move with the villain still under instruction. After about two miles of erratic driving, things started to calm down and we headed for the Blackwall Tunnel. We were Essex-bound. At the first roadside café, the lorry pulled in to meet the white van, out jumped the real driver who climbed into the van, and his place was taken by villain number two. Then Jacko hopped into another stolen car and we all set off.

After about one hour and forty minutes, the lorry pulled into an industrial park on the outskirts of Colchester where five men were waiting. Right on cue Jacko drove in and took over the proceedings. The lorry doors were thrown open, and he and another man climbed in the back to examine the contents. Obviously satisfied, the two men shook hands and a big fat roll of money found its way into Jacko's grasping hands. It was time to go to work. Our cars screeched in from every conceivable angle, and chaos reigned for a few minutes until the thieves and the receivers were safely handcuffed and sitting comfortably in the back of police cars. Then we realized the man that handed the money to Jacko was missing.

Somebody shouted and pointed to a Jaguar car disappearing out of the car park. Two of our cars gave chase, giving the prisoners handcuffed in the back the first-hand experience of a police chase and capture. For some reason they didn't seem to be enjoying their time with us.

With everything safe and the stolen lorry taken away to be restored to its rightful owners, it was time to get down to the paperwork. The prisoners had all been taken to Colchester Police Station where the desk sergeant realized his normal late-turn shift was about to turn into a long one. With seven prisoners in his cells, he was about to be burdened with preparing charge sheets, arranging refreshments, dealing with solicitors, arranging bail, and a host of related enquiries from family, friends and the inevitable newspaper reporter who just happened to be passing and wondered why there was so much activity.

Our team was assembled, and we were assigned our respective prisoners to interview and process so that they could appear for a preliminary hearing at the magistrates' court the following morning. It would be two or three months before the case could be sent to the crown court and another six to nine months before the actual trial would take place.

The case was easy enough to put together. There was no problem convincing Jacko that it was the stupidity of his driver that led to their arrest. This meant that the only statement we needed from the actual lorry driver was a brief description of his kidnap. As he was the informant, he was off the hook, and relieved to know that he could say he didn't recognize anyone and so be free of the reprisals he so feared.

The detective inspector decided which officers would interview which prisoner, and Dave and I were given the prisoner who had nearly made good his escape. Walking into the interview room that evening, I didn't realize that I was just starting out on the busiest and most successful year of my career so far.

Expecting to be confronted by a typical East End wide boy, we were pleasantly surprised to be met by a polite, well-manicured man of about 25 whose name was James. Standing up, he offered his hand and said, 'Good evening officers. How can I be of assistance to you?' He said he understood he was in rather a difficult predicament and asked if £2,000 would make his problems diminish somewhat. We explained that it might well get him a better lawyer. He smiled and said that wasn't exactly what he had in mind, but there must be a price we could agree upon that would be beneficial to him. Gently, we said he had been watching too many movies as every 'cop film' assumed or implied that all police were bent. We were, however, always willing to help reduce his prison time and if he was prepared to provide us with information, the better that would be for him. James explained that he had never been arrested before and wasn't sure of the procedure, but that he was very sorry, he could never be an informer.

We sat down to start the process of charging him and taking his antecedent history. He told us he had five other businesses and was a very rich man. 'Why on earth are you doing this?' asked Dave. James explained that it wasn't the money, but simply the adrenaline rush and the thrill of the chase. A couple of hours later the paperwork was completed and James was released on bail to appear at the local magistrates' court in three weeks' time. Then it was down the local pub for a well-earned drink with the rest of the team.

Over a couple of pints, each pair shared their stories. The two detectives who interviewed Jacko were amused by the fact he had done nothing, but curse the driver he had recruited for his inability to drive a 'fucking artic'. We all wondered how long it would be before the driver was found battered and bruised in some back alley in Peckham. Dave and I didn't have much to say about James, but we both had a feeling that we'd see more of him in the future.

Three weeks later, at the first remand hearing, we were approached by James who apologized for insulting us by making such a miserly offer for our co-operation and doubled it to £4,000. Again we politely declined and explained to him that if he worked for us he would not only get his much-needed adrenaline rush, but he would also earn a few pounds from the informants' fund as well as the insurance reward for recovered property. For the second time we reached an impasse.

Roll on another three weeks and we were back at court for committal proceedings, which would see the case referred to the crown court for trial. As we left court James walked past and shook my hand, leaving behind a piece of paper requesting us to meet him at a café in east London. Meeting someone on bail without getting permission from a senior officer was taboo. And this was shortly after the new commissioner of the Metropolitan Police, Robert Mark, had been to his first meeting with the Flying Squad. It was the shortest meeting I had ever attended. Mark walked in the room and said, 'You're all bent', and walked out. What a wonderful incentive for officers who were working seventy or eighty hours a week dealing with the most prolific and dangerous criminals in London.

We duly made our phone call and got permission to meet James, although we were concerned that he might be setting us up. We were worried that we would sit down and an envelope would be pushed across the table stuffed with money, and from out of the woodwork would appear a team of incorruptible senior uniform officers who had been tasked to arrest any Squad officers for any irregularity or infringement. Sounds crazy, but the purge of the Flying Squad was at its peak. So Dave and I agreed we would be the monkeys that saw everything, heard everything, but said nothing and touched nothing. The next move was down to James.

We joined James at a table against the back wall of the cafe, making sure we could see the front door. James stood up, shook hands and said, 'Time to talk?' We ordered a full English breakfast and a cup of coffee. 'I suppose,' said James, 'there's no chance of us reaching any agreement, other than me working for you?' We shook our heads. 'Okay,' he said smiling. 'Let's give it a try.'

The next couple of hours were taken up with us explaining the dos and don'ts of his new career, then contact details were exchanged and we agreed that the only place we would ever meet would be this café. James said that it wasn't only his life that was changing, but ours as well, as any information he gave us was likely to be about five in the morning and we would need to be ready to act before seven.

We left James and proceeded to New Scotland Yard where more paperwork was required to register him as an informant. Up until the arrival of Mark, an informant's identity was known only to the officers who recruited and used him, and many officers refused to name their informants, even under cross-examination in court. However, a study implemented by the commissioner had determined that this was unhealthy and the identity of informants should be recorded on a special form, which would be held securely in the commander's safe. Every meeting between the officers and informant had to be requested and noted on the form, together with the information passed on. Each informant would be given a pseudonym. We decided on Chester for James purely and simply because Colchester had been where we first met.

Over the years, some officers got too close to their informants and formed unhealthy relationships, which resulted in corruption. The most notable case concerned Commander Ken Drury, the former head of the Flying Squad, who served eight years in prison for accepting a luxury Cyprus holiday paid for by Jimmy Humphreys, the king of Soho's pornography operation (Drury's alibi was he was looking for Ronnie Biggs). It was most probably this event that caused Mark to tar every squad detective with the same brush, but the new draconian measures regarding the handling of informants was, in many officers' opinions, the start of the demise of the CID and the Flying Squad in particular. Many informants stopped co-operating with officers when they learned that details would now be noted down, and so much good information was lost. Nothing is truer than the saying that a secret is something only two share (or three when officers worked in pairs).

A senior officer called David Powis had been selected to oversee these new procedures and declared himself a figurehead for the fight against corruption. He introduced new rules and regulations that were simply farcical. For example, he decided that when an informant was to be paid a reasonably large sum of money, he would do it personally. Powis would direct the officer handling the informant to bring him (or occasionally her) to an appointed location near Scotland Yard, always after dark. There, he would introduce himself and, using the informant's pseudonym, give him a five-minute lecture about the money he was about to receive, that it was British taxpayers' money and its receipt was not to be treated lightly. He would then praise the informant and ask for his continued contributions to the never-ending fight against crime. This would be followed by an announcement that this money was for him and him alone, and under no circumstances should it be shared with 'that man', and point to the officer. Then he would hand over the money and the informant would sign a receipt using his pseudonym.

Treating the informant as if he were some long-lost son, Powis would ask personal questions without realizing that he never got an honest answer. His parting words would be that he was the highest-ranking detective in London and he would know if any breach of his instructions occurred. This came from an officer who had never been a detective before this appointment. He was so pompous and I don't think it ever occurred to him that, if the informant and the officer were going to share the reward money, they would just meet down the pub or somewhere else at a later date.

These pantomime performances became known as 'crazy hour' and it wasn't long before Powis earned the nickname 'Crazy Horse', which he carried for the remainder of his career.

With all the paperwork completed, it was time to sit back and wait for our first call from the newly-named Chester. A couple of days later at 5.00 am, I was awakened by the telephone, and given the registration number and location of a van loaded with stolen goods. Immediately, two cars, two drivers and four officers raced to London. The van was located and, after pulling it over, we discovered we'd recovered stolen property amounting to four cases of bananas, three of satsumas, two of oranges, and the same again of strawberries and raspberries. The whole lot amounted to a wholesale value of about £120. Not very impressed, we quickly charged the driver with theft at the local police station and took him to the magistrates' court where he pleaded guilty, was fined £50 and sent on his way.

Later that afternoon Chester called and we met at the designated café. He apologized and said he just wanted to see if the system worked. We had a heated discussion about him wasting our time and we didn't leave the café on the best of terms. The following Tuesday the phone went again at the same ungodly hour with similar instructions. This time it was a *little* better and it was meat: four lambs, a side of beef, four cases of vacuum–packed fillet, two boxes of frozen burgers and two cases of liver. It was worth almost £300 and was followed by court, a fine and back to the yard to attend a hastily-convened team meeting. Dave and I were told that should anyone be dragged out of bed for any lorry that didn't contain something akin to the crown jewels, the next box of liver would be spread over our heads and those of the 'bloody informants'. We demanded an immediate meeting with Chester. He said he knew we were upset, but he couldn't meet us until Tuesday next week. We had no option but to agree.

The following Tuesday we arrived at the cafe to see Chester sitting at his table with his hands in the air, as if he were surrendering. 'Okay,' he said. 'I needed to be sure. Those two were just practice runs. I had to be certain that there was no comeback on me, that nobody suspected me and that you haven't taken a bung. Everything is cool so now we can go to work. If that's okay with you.' He said there'd be a 'ton of work' coming our way starting with a refrigerated lorry heading to Billingsgate Fish Market this Friday. We were furious with him for messing us around, but what could we do but agree?

Once outside, Dave looked at me and shook his head. 'Did that really just happen?' he asked. 'We've just been put on trial by a bloody villain to see if we are trustworthy.' We returned to the team and asked for one more chance.

True to his word Chester delivered. We stopped the lorry on the A1 about thirty-five miles outside of London. Sure enough, the vehicle full of fish had been stolen in the middle of the night from Grimsby Docks.

This was the start of twelve months of unbelievable success. Chester delivered stolen lorry loads of everything, from whisky to cigarettes, and all types of fresh and frozen produce, including tulips from Amsterdam.

We even intercepted a lorry load of Manx kippers, but we had to wait two weeks for it as the fish were still being smoked. It was difficult to keep up with him and our lives slipped into a routine of early-morning calls, stopping lorries, searching premises, and dealing with high and low-value loads. It became necessary for us to rent our own cold storage unit and we had our own insurance assessor at the end of a phone courtesy of the Road Haulage Association. It was his job to try and sell the recovered property while it was still fresh.

We managed to delay Chester's trial for as long as possible, but after about fifteen months it took place at Chelmsford Crown Court. A letter signed by the commissioner, detailing Chester's help over the past year had been delivered to the judge, but obviously at the point of sentence all the defendants had to be treated in the same way. They were all found guilty and sentenced to five years' imprisonment, except for Jacko who was adjudged to be the leader, and he got an extra twelve months.

Chester's girlfriend called us that evening and said the only words he'd spoken were 'where was the bloody help?' We explained that he would have to wait a few weeks otherwise it would be obvious to everyone that he was an informant. Four weeks later he was moved to an open prison and his sentence was reduced to eighteen months. The girlfriend's next phone call was simply a thank you. Chester was released ten months later and immediately arranged a meeting with us. Arriving at the café, we found him in peak physical condition, having done nothing, but play sport and work out in the gym during his time inside. We sat down and ordered the statutory full English, but after regaling us with stories about his incarceration he said, 'That's it. You won't be hearing from me again unless it's for breakfast.' As we said our goodbyes, he climbed into his new car and drove off to his country estate where he continued to lead a comfortable life amassing his (legitimate) fortune. It was nice to be able to sleep past dawn for a change.

One day in early May 1973, an inspector from another team requested our help on an operation. They had information regarding an armed robbery on a cash-in-transit security vehicle delivering to a bank in the

London suburb of Surbiton. The raid was scheduled to take place at 11.00 am on the coming Friday and our team's part was back-up in case things went wrong at the scene and extra troops were needed. At the briefing early on Friday morning, everyone was given their positions and by 7.00 am I was ensconced in a pitch-black basement boiler room at the rear of the bank. The light bulbs had been removed to ensure that if the robbers *reconnoitred* the scene, they would see nothing of me hidden behind the boiler. With a truncheon in one hand and a walkie-talkie between my feet, I sat on a wooden box and stared into the blackness knowing that it would be four hours before I saw daylight again. Apart from a quick message every fifteen minutes or so from the officer controlling the operation to ensure that we were awake, it was just a case of sitting there wondering what would have happened if you'd turned left instead of right at some earlier point in your life. 'What if?' is a great way to while away a few hours.

Just after 10.30 am the radio crackled into life: the villains had been seen driving round the area checking to make sure there was no police presence. The commentary intensified as the security vehicle got closer to the bank, and I started to sweat, fidget and breathe quicker as the adrenaline kicked in. 'Standby!' said the voice over the radio. 'Standby! It's going to happen guys. Good luck.' I waited a few seconds and then it came: 'Go! Go! Go!' I ran up the stairs. My job was simply to get to the front of the bank as quickly as possible. Opening the door and turning left, I started to run, but after sitting for hours in total darkness the bright sunlight was blinding. I ran down the side of the building towards the front and then collided at full speed with a man running in the opposite direction. We fell to the ground in a tangle of arms and legs. My vision was still quite hazy and, looking down, I noticed the person I had knocked to the floor had a walking stick. Feeling guilty at having upended an elderly gentleman, I was poised to apologize when I glanced down again. With my 20/20 vision now fully restored, I saw that the walking stick was actually two sticks that looked remarkably like the barrels of a sawn-off shotgun. My brain just about registered what was lying beneath me when the two of us became six as other officers dived into the scrum. 'Well done,' they shouted into my ear as they relieved the robber of his weapon, handcuffed him and led him away.

In November the following year, I stood with three other Flying Squad officers at London County Hall as we were presented with the Queen's Commendation for Brave Conduct by Her Majesty's Lord–Lieutenant of Greater London. As I stood there, listening to the citation being read by the newly-knighted Sir Robert Mark, it struck me as rather ironic that the last time I had heard him speak was when he told me and 100 other officers that we were all corrupt. After a couple of cucumber sandwiches, a cup of coffee and a fairy cake, I left with my family, who were the only people who knew my secret of what could only be described as my own version of blind man's bluff. I was honoured to receive the award, but I did feel a tad guilty, as though I didn't really deserve it.

The average length of a posting to the Flying Squad was about four years as it had been established that after that length of time the officers were starting to face burn out. I had been there for three years and eight months, and was coming towards the end of my tenure when, a couple of weeks after the award ceremony, an event that could be interpreted as either good or bad luck stopped me in my tracks.

On 24 November 1974, my car was in the garage awaiting repair so I took my wife's Fiat 500 to work. It been a long day and we didn't clock off until the early hours of the morning. It was snowing as I began the twenty-five-mile drive back to the Kent suburbs and I was almost home when I lost control of the car. Although seatbelts were fitted in all vehicles, it was not yet compulsory to wear them and, for some reason, I had not put mine on that night. As the car started to spin, my eyes were drawn to a lamp post which appeared to be moving directly into my path.

I knew that we were on a collision course so I lay down across the passenger seat and put my hands on my head, a feat I would have never been able to accomplish had I been wearing the safety belt. The car hit the lamp post head on and the steering wheel went out through the roof.

The floor well split open and my feet went through on to the road. A couple more spins and the car came to rest.

A couple of miles up the road at my home, something strange happened. My wife Beth, normally a good sleeper, had, for some reason, woken and come downstairs. Looking out of the window, she saw a panda car drive past and then moments later it came back. The local officer came up and knocked on the door. He explained that I had been involved in an accident and that the emergency services were still trying to get me out of the car. In true British fashion, she made a cup of tea for them both and they sat in the kitchen awaiting further news. The next radio message was not the one she wanted to hear. It said: 'We've got him out. He's on the way to Bromley Hospital, but it looks like a fatal.' My wife knocked on our next-door neighbour's door. He was also a detective sergeant and, in a few minutes, they were on their way to hospital.

My good luck had prevailed. Although I was drifting in and out of consciousness, the main damage was below the waist. I had two broken legs and the left foot, which had been dragged along the ground, was torn to shreds with most of the bones broken. After a couple of days in intensive care, I was visited by an orthopaedic surgeon and his registrar. The surgeon explained that it was likely my foot would be amputated, but that the registrar would be taking over and that he would make the decision at the appropriate time. The registrar then sat down with me and asked what I did for a living. I told him I was a police officer and he asked what opportunities there would be for me at work if my foot were to be removed. I drew a blank and he said he would see me in the morning. The following day I was taken to the operating theatre where each of the bones in my foot was reset one by one. I was later to learn from his wife that the night before he operated, he spent the evening at home with my X-rays on the kitchen table and drew a detailed plan of how to save my foot. Many operations later, with certain parts of my anatomy being transferred to my foot, I was able to gaze down at my newly-shaped four-toed foot. Eight months later, I returned to work, something I could not have done if it hadn't been for the care and skill of one man.

During my recovery, the camaraderie of the squad was never more evident and appreciated. Every senior officer from the commander down visited at some point. Each of the officers made a contribution from their weekly expenses, which was given to my wife together with a bouquet of flowers. When I had to go to London for treatment, a car and driver would be designated to ensure Beth could visit.

A couple of months after going back to work, the inevitable transfer arrived and I was off to Greenwich to take my place in an everyday CID office. I left with great sadness, but with many happy memories of the most enjoyable period of my career so far.

Chapter 8

Lucky Buggers

Greenwich Police Station in Royal Hill is a building of no particular architectural interest and is not the most pleasing to the eye. It stands a few streets back from the Thames and from the top floor the view includes the historical tea clipper *Cutty Sark*, which sits in a dry dock in King William Walk. The station area is one of the more affluent in London, but also includes the council estates on the Deptford borders. Greenwich is also frequented by tourists who are visiting the Royal Observatory, the National Maritime Museum and the O2 Arena (formerly the Millennium Dome). Police work here is as diversified as anywhere else in the capital with everything from burglary to domestic violence, weekend punch-ups and an increasing recreational drug problem in the emerging wine bars. The tourists attract the pickpockets and thieves who work in gangs, and come from all over the city for the easy pickings presented to them.

The slower pace of life enabled me to study for the inspectors' exam and, true to form, I managed to secure a pass. I was saved the ignominy of being the last name on the printed list of successful candidates purely because my surname starts with a letter at the start of the alphabet.

One morning, Detective Chief Superintendent Charlie Snape called me into his office and told me I was to go with him to meet an informant of his who was incarcerated in a prison in Kent. Charlie was a 'copper's copper'. He had served on the Flying Squad on a number of occasions and was the epitome of a squad officer. It didn't matter how many times they were promoted they all hated sitting behind a desk and, if it wasn't for the money, would willingly go back to being a detective sergeant just to get some action. Charlie treated everyone the same, be he copper or criminal; his word was his bond and he was respected on both sides of the fence. His informants were loyal to him and him alone; hence the man we were going to see had refused to speak to anyone except Charlie.

In prison, we listened to conversations the informant had overheard from a fellow prisoner who boasted that while he was only doing nine months for 'taking and driving away' (a car), he should really be doing a seven-year stretch for armed robbery. He had been telling all and sundry that he had actually been the getaway driver at the first changeover point for a gang of armed robbers. He said his team had carried out a robbery less than a mile from where he had been arrested, but the police were out of their car questioning him and hadn't heard the call regarding the robbery. His audience was in stitches when he said he saw the robbers drive past with cash and guns in their car, grinning and waving. He went on to give extraordinary details about the gang, explaining that they committed one or two crimes a month up and down the country, and always struck on a Thursday as this was the day the security vehicles were fully loaded with cash required for Friday's payday or money being moved by the banks before the end of the week They called themselves the 'Thursday gang' and although he was careful not to identify any of the gang by their real names, he was stupid enough to mention a few nicknames. The informant told us that the leader was 'Top Cat', that 'Big Jim' was a 'vicious evil bastard' and 'Benny' was not popular, but he had plenty of bottle.

On the way back to Greenwich, the governor had a big smile on his face and told me that if this worked out he could be back having fun all over again. The first job, however, would be to identify the crimes and put together the most likely team of robbers. It was time to earn our corn. Together with Ray, a young detective constable, we acquired the file of the big-mouthed prisoner and extracted the names of all his associates, then all their associates and so on until we had the names of fifty or so active criminals. We identified a robbery at Rochester, which had taken place while the prisoner was being arrested, and fifteen similar robberies as far north as the ICI works at Billingham in Durham and as far south as Plymouth. The most recent, in Banstead, Surrey, happened only a few days earlier.

'Top Cat' was almost certainly Charlie Knight, a well-known east London robber also known as 'Chopper' or 'The Guvnor'. 'Big Jim' was definitely Jim Moody who was, indeed, a vicious evil bastard. He went back to the days of the Richardsons where, together with 'Mad' Frankie Fraser, he had carried out beatings and torture of people who had crossed the Richardson gang. Next was 'Benny', who was easily identified as Sammy Benifield. It wasn't long before we put a team of ten to fifteen robbers together. All were known to the police and were mid-thirties or older. It was a formidable list.

Witnesses at the Banstead robbery had described a large man dressed as a police officer who, armed with a shotgun, had stood in the middle of the A3 and held up traffic. As he turned to walk back to his police car, the gun had gone off and he shot himself in the foot. He had hobbled back to his car and made his getaway in a cloud of burning rubber. We bet this was Moody.

Armed with this information, Charlie went to Scotland Yard where he convinced senior officers that, as it was his informant, he would be the best person to put together a team of officers to try and apprehend these prolific robbers. Much to the annoyance of the Flying Squad, who were dealing with the Banstead robbery, Charlie was given the go ahead to assemble officers from all the forces that had suffered a robbery from this team and Operation Ohio was born. Charlie's second in command was from Kent and his operational head was another good old Flying Squad officer, a well-respected dour Scotsman named Bill Foreman. With a nucleus of Met officers, a control centre and office was set up at the little-used Westcombe Park Police Station, close to the Blackwall Tunnel. Officers were seconded from each of the police forces that had been victims of this team.

In every inquiry, there must be an office manager and an intelligence officer. It is their job to read everything, collate it, evaluate it, report to the chief and then reassign enquiries from that information. I got the job of intelligence officer (this term should not in any way be confused with that of intelligent officer).

At the start of any inquiry, the enthusiasm is at its zenith and to keep that level you desperately need an early success. Our biggest problem was that although we had identified three of the potential robbers, none of them had been seen for at least three years. Benny was among those who had vanished, but, after examining his file, we found one constant in his history. That was his wife/girlfriend, a woman called Edith who had a good job and no criminal convictions, and we had an address for her. Two female detectives were dispatched to watch her, and on the first Friday they followed her to a Chinese restaurant where she met a girlfriend and enjoyed a meal, which she paid for on credit card. The officers persuaded the owner to give them the details of the credit card and a scroll through the transactions revealed that every second Friday she hired a car for the weekend, returning it Monday morning. A check was made with Avis and, sure enough, Edith had a car reserved for pick-up at 6.00 pm the following Friday.

A phone call to C11, the intelligence department at Scotland Yard, reserved a surveillance team for the coming Friday. So when Edith picked up her rental car and set off, she was completely unaware that behind her were a couple of motorbikes, a van and a couple of cars from C11. Behind them were officers from Operation Ohio who were listening on the police radio. As she left London and crossed the border to Surrey, she pulled into a parade of shops and purchased a large carrier bag of takeaway Chinese food. Another two miles in the car and she turned into *The Roof of the World* caravan park at Box Hill, Tadworth. This well-established park had room for touring caravans, but was mostly laid out to accommodate long-term residents in static mobile homes. She obviously knew her way around, and it wasn't long before she pulled into the drive of a green mobile home and out the front door walked a smiling Sammy Benifield.

Charlie thought it might be prudent to give them an hour to themselves, by which time they would have most probably finished eating and adjourned to the bedroom for dessert. If they were naked, they were less likely to resist arrest. We also needed the time to obtain a search warrant. Just over an hour later an officer arrived with the warrant and it was time to say hi to Benny. The front door gave way easily and, as it crashed to the ground, officers poured in. It proved to be a good call from the boss. As we entered the bedroom, Benny leaped naked from the bed and, trying to run, got tangled up in his trousers, which had been discarded on the floor, and fell flat on his face. He got to his feet and half climbed out the window, but was pushed back in by the officers who were surrounding the back of the premises. Lying on the floor, defeated and naked, he looked up at us and said, 'Evening all.'

A thorough search of his home revealed his unusual method of insulation: bank notes amounting to £83,000 stuffed behind the wall panels. After all the photographs had been taken and forensic evidence collected, it was time for Benny to say goodbye to Edith and his freedom, and make the biggest decision of his life. Almost immediately he decided he couldn't face any more long prison sentences and he asked for a deal. Confessing to more than forty robberies, he proceeded to name all his accomplices. But one man's word is never enough, so we had to track down more of the robbers on our list.

One of the names we had was a well-known criminal called John Segars who was involved with the most recent robbery at Banstead. He was traced and arrested with his wife in a guesthouse in Minehead, Somerset. Segars didn't want to talk, but his family did and quickly told the officers that he kept his ill-gotten gains in two suitcases at his Aunt Sally's house in west London. Racing to the address, Bill asked Aunt Sally where the suitcases were. 'Under the bed in the spare room,' was the reply. Bill found the suitcases, brought them down and opened them in front of her. They were both stuffed full of bundles of bank notes. Aunt Sally took one look, said 'Fucking hell' and fainted. Over £84,000 was recovered. Charlie took the suitcases to Banstead Police Station and showed them to Segars. His response was similar to Aunt Sally's, but for a different reason. Charlie gave him ten minutes to make a decision. Tell everything and get five years, keep quiet and get fifteen. Segars didn't need his full quota of allotted time before making up his mind. Throwing his hands in the air he said, 'Fuck it. I've had enough.'

Over the next few days, Segars admitted to almost forty robberies and, again, gave us names, dates, and every minute detail of planning and execution. Now we had two villains corroborating each other, we had enough. All that remained was to find them and arrest them.

In the 1970s, the most prevalent serious crime was bank robbery and armed attacks on cash-carrying security vehicles. The largest bank robbery to date occurred at a branch of Barclays Bank in Ilford where thieves escaped with £237,000. The team was led by Derek Creighton Smalls, better known as 'Bertie Smalls' and, after they made their escape, they left the country to enjoy the sunshine in the newly-established villains' playground, the Costa del Sol, Spain. This destination had become popular, not just for the weather, but because Spain had no extradition treaty with the UK.

A police informant had named Smalls as the leader of the gang, but the Flying Squad was unable to locate him. After a year of police officers swooping in and searching the homes of his family and friends on a regular basis, Smalls called the police to offer a deal. He would give himself up, name every job he and his team had committed, name every person who had taken part and turn Queen's evidence (grass them up) at their trials. In return he would serve no prison time and receive a new identity. Furthermore, he wanted the deal in writing.

A meeting was arranged with Director of Public Prosecutions Sir Norman Skelhorn, who agreed to the terms. Smalls duly gave evidence, which resulted in 308 years' imprisonment being handed down to twenty-one of his former friends. At one of the committal hearings, his former associates regaled the judiciary with a raucous rendition of Vera Lynn's *We'll Meet Again* for the entire time Smalls was talking. He is considered to be Britain's first supergrass. However, in the aftermath, the Law Lords informed the director of public prosecutions they considered this arrangement with Smalls an 'unholy deal', which should not be repeated.

In 1974, prolific robber Maurice O'Mahoney supplied the police with the names of more than 150 criminals and had his twenty-year sentence slashed to five. This was spent in police custody while he gave both information to the police and evidence to the courts. Five or six years became the recognized tariff for future supergrasses.

Back at Westcombe Park, with both Benny and Segars fully debriefed and the myriad information they had provided in over eighty statements collated and examined, it was time to locate the robbers. One by one they were found and kept under observation ready for the big round up ,but two – Jim Moody and Tony Knightley – were proving to be elusive. All we knew was that they communicated to the rest of their team from a telephone box and they each had a static mobile home on the same site, somewhere on the coast, possibly in Bournemouth. It was close to a marina in a small village, it was near a pub and Moody was 'trying to pull the bird next door'.

Four officers were dispatched to search the coast from Bournemouth to Weymouth. They came back empty of information, but full of beer having managed to visit every village and every pub along the way.

A couple of days later, Charlie called me to his office and said, 'You're a lucky bugger. Want to have a go at finding them?' What a wonderful reputation to have. Not 'you're a good detective,' just, 'you're a lucky bugger!' The trouble was, it was the truth. So it was agreed that I would 'go camping' with one other officer, Detective Sergeant Alan Wall from Cleveland. We agreed to meet at my house on Sunday morning. I sat reading the Sunday papers and browsing the supplements until Alan arrived. With a cheery 'See you sometime,' and a wave to the family, we set off in my car for the sunny south coast.

'Any idea where they might be?' Alan asked. 'Absolutely none,' was my reply. However, in the Sunday supplement I read that Ted Heath kept his yacht '*Morning Cloud*' moored at a marina in Hamble, near Southampton, and thought it would be as good a place to start as any. About ninety minutes later we were sitting on the dockside watching Heath's yacht bobbing up and down on the incoming tide. After thirty minutes, we decided to journey on. Leaving the marina, we turned left and immediately in front of us was a sign that said Riverside Park, Caravanning & Camping. Entering the site, we saw a Range Rover with its bonnet raised and two men working on the engine. We drove past, looked at each other and burst out laughing. The two men were Moody and Knightley. Alan looked at me and said, 'The governor told me you were lucky, but that's ridiculous.'

We turned round and drove to the local country policeman's house at Eastleigh, which was also the police station. Our first request was to use the telephone to speak to Detective Chief Superintendent Snape at his home in London. His reply to our cheery 'Good morning' was, 'I thought you had gone on your holidays.' I said, 'Turns out to be a short break Guv. We've found them both together in Hampshire.' It took a while to convince him this was true. Then he said he'd given everyone Sunday off so we were instructed to keep them under surveillance until early the following morning when a team of officers would be with us. He would ensure the local police were aware of events and would, he hoped, be in the vicinity to help if necessary. He would try to get two officers to join us later that day. His parting words were, 'Well done both of you. By the way you have got to be the luckiest bugger I have ever met.'

We asked the local officer for a copy of *The Police Gazette*, a nationwide publication that published photos of criminals wanted throughout the UK. On the front page were the 'most wanted' and in position number one was an old photo of Moody. We asked the local officer to phone the manager of the caravan park and ask him to come to the station without telling anyone. Ten minutes later he arrived and confirmed that the photo was a man called Jim Bryant, and that he and his friend Tony had each rented a park home for a year. They had been there for eleven months and were in the process of renewing the rental for a further year. The homes were next door but one to each other and in the middle lived a young Australian woman called Sue. He thought that Jim and Sue had recently become more than just neighbours. It was arranged that in about an hour, we would come to his office and rent a caravan.

We moved into our new home and waited for reinforcements. About 6.00 pm, Moody came out, casually dressed, and drove away in his Range Rover. We felt there wasn't anything to worry about as his clothing indicated that he was just going somewhere local, probably to do a bit of shopping. Unfortunately, without our knowledge, two local officers saw him drive into a supermarket some ten miles away and, contrary to instructions, had decided to arrest him. Approaching Moody resulted in the two officers being knocked to the floor and Moody disappearing in a cloud of dust. All we could do was hope that as this incident took place quite far away, Moody would not think his home had been compromised and would return, even if just to collect his belongings. A criminal of his stature would be prepared for most eventualities and would almost certainly have another set of false number plates to put on his vehicle.

A couple of hours later, we were joined by two more officers who had travelled from London. As each hour passed, the chances of Moody returning diminished, but the good news was we had seen Knightley a couple of times so all was not lost. At 1.00 am, Knightley came out of his house carrying a Gladstone bag, got in his car and drove away. We had lost one, but no way were we losing both so we jumped into my car and set off in pursuit. Radio contact was made with the local officers and a road block was set up three miles away. Knightley quickly realized he was being followed and increased his speed to about 70mph, which in the country lanes of Hampshire was plenty fast enough. As he came round a corner he was confronted with a local panda car heading towards him. He didn't slow down so the officer in the panda had to make a self-preservation manoeuvre by turning sharp right into a field full of sheep without bothering to open the gate. Another mile, another corner and this time two police cars were sitting nose to nose to block the road. Knightley ploughed in to them, blasting them out of the way. In the collision, the bonnet of Knightley's car flew up, covering his windscreen and his door flew off. He still didn't slow down.

For the next few miles he continued to drive at breakneck speeds, hanging out of the empty door frame to see where he was going. We followed at a safe distance as he sped through the narrow lanes until we reached the village of Netley. In a flash of blue light, a patrol car passed us and pulled up alongside Knightley. His response was immediate: applying the brakes he slowed just enough to turn right behind the police car and head down a track towards the sea. As he came to the sea wall, his car took off and landed nose first in three feet of mud and water. Knightley leapt from the vehicle, dived in to the sea and swam out into the moonlit Southampton Water. We clambered down to shore to see two boys of about 14-years-old standing with their mouths open and fishing rods in their hands.

Of the four of us, none were stupid enough or brave enough to join Knightley in his swim for freedom. Instead we opened the boot of his car and found the Gladstone bag stuffed full of bank notes. A few minutes later we were joined by the head of Hampshire CID. He was fuming. 'Sweeney come down here, mess up an easy arrest of two robbers, write off three of my police cars, put two of my officers in hospital. What a night.' We should have stayed silent, but Alan decided to pipe up and say, 'The good thing is Sir, we are on your side.' It was definitely time to leave.

Sitting in the caravan in the middle of the night, soaking wet and with mud up to our waist, we were aware of our total failure. A day that had started out so positively, by locating two of England's most wanted criminals, had ended with one lost and one possibly drowned. The only thing we had to show for our endeavours was a Gladstone bag full of money, which, when counted later, was more than £78,000. The coast guard told us that nobody had ever swum across Southampton Water; the currents were far too strong, especially on an ebb tide. Nobody could survive; certainly not someone who was fully clothed and still had his boots on.

It was time to return to London with our tails between our legs, but not before we'd interviewed Sue, the Australian lady friend of Moody's. It took a couple of hours to gain her confidence, and for her to come to terms with who and what the Jim she knew really was. Eventually she told us about their relationship and the first thing she said was that, due to an incident that had occurred that morning, she had decided not to spend any more time with him.

She had met Jim six months earlier when she had moved into her mobile home with her husband. Her marriage was in difficulty, and three months later they split and he left. Both Moody and Knightley had been very kind to her in the aftermath of her marriage breakdown. She was a person who, for whatever reason, maintained a very comprehensive diary. Moody had told her he was a long-distance lorry driver and this accounted for his frequent days of absence. Unfortunately for him, the dates of his away days were recorded in Sue's diary and examination of her notes found they coincided every time with a Thursday robbery. On one of these Thursdays, Jim had returned home limping badly. Sue had examined his foot and treated a large wound, which he claimed (but she doubted) happened when he stood on some nails sticking out of a pallet while loading his lorry. She had tried to make him go to hospital, but he refused and got abusive when she tried to insist. A check on this date showed it coincided with the Banstead robbery, when one of the robbers had mistakenly discharged his shotgun and literally shot himself in the foot. If only we could get Moody in the dock, it would be a wonderful piece of evidence to present to the court.

Sue then told us why she had decided to end her relationship with Moody. Over the last few weeks, their friendship had become sexual and on two occasions she spent the night with him, the last time being the Saturday just gone. Everything had been fine until they woke up on Sunday morning and were sat reading the papers when Sue remarked on a report about an elderly woman being strangled. Without warning, Moody stood up and said, 'It's easy to strangle someone.' Then he had crossed the room, put his giant hands around her neck and strangled her, causing her to pass out. When she regained consciousness, he was sitting back in his chair, calmly reading the paper. Looking up he said casually, 'I could have killed you if I'd wanted to.' Shaking, and with tears streaming down her face, she removed a scarf from round her neck and revealed a complete set of fingerprint bruises, with two clear thumb prints over her Adam's apple. She quickly made an excuse to leave, but was terrified of telling him she wouldn't see him anymore. Now that we had told her she was caught up with one of the country's most wanted criminals, she decided she needed to get as far away from him as possible. A couple of weeks later, Sue was sailing away from Southampton on her way back to Australia.

The following morning, a woman reported seeing a wet and bedraggled man come ashore on the other side of Southampton Water at Fawley Power Station. Incredibly, he still had his shoes round his neck. When interviewed later, he told us that he had managed to swim from one moored boat to the next until he had to cross the main shipping channel. It had taken him over eight hours to negotiate his journey and he felt lucky to have survived. However, his good fortune came to an end when he appeared with other members of his team at Maidstone Crown Court, charged with committing armed robberies, which had netted them almost £2 million. They were all found guilty and between them received prison sentences totalling 218 years. Knightley was sentenced to ten years and the leader, Charlie 'Top Cat' Knight, got eighteen. Operation Ohio had drawn to a wonderful conclusion, but only one thing needed resolving. Where was Jim Moody?

Our sighting of Moody in Hamble, with his head in the bonnet of a Range Rover, was in 1978 and this was the first recorded time he had been seen by police since his release from prison in 1973. He was a giant in the criminal world, having been locked up in Borstal from the age of 17. These custodial young offenders' prisons were intended to instil discipline, and set the men on a path towards a productive and crime-free future. Instead, they offered a two-year course on every type of criminal enterprise known to man. Moody was already a thief and a burglar who could steal cars in minutes, and he was violent, beating senseless anyone who got in his way. On completion of his incarceration he came back to his parental home in Camberwell, south London, where his mother attempted to put him on the straight and narrow by persuading him to join the Merchant Navy.

His career on the high seas ended with a seaman's book containing six 'declined reports' for fighting, These are the Navy's equivalent of a warning; two of these make it almost impossible to find a ship and with six, you're unemployable. So, back in London, not yet 20-years-old, violent and jobless, he came to the attention of the South London gang the Richardsons, aka the 'torture gang', which was run by brothers Eddie and Charlie Richardson. They had their finger in every criminal enterprise in South-East London and hired 'enforcers', people who would hand out punishment to miscreants who failed to abide by the Richardsons' creed of conduct. Their chief enforcer was 'Mad' Frankie Fraser who was reputed to be the most violent man in London. But there was too much work for him so they gave a trial to Moody, who proved himself invaluable and was taken on as Fraser's right-hand man.

The violence inflicted by these men was appalling. Fraser's weapon of choice was a pair of pliers with which he would extract teeth from his victims. Moody's preference was a hammer, used to break the bones of people's feet. It was not uncommon for them to beat a man unconscious, and then have a sandwich and a cup of tea while the victim recovered enough for the torture to continue.

Moody was also used by the Richardsons for jury tampering. For a fee, jurors in a trial could be visited and persuaded to bring in a not-guilty verdict. Moody just had to knock on a juror's door to ensure the trial reached the required result. His reputation became such that he was being linked to every act of extreme violence or gangland execution that happened in London.

On 7 February 1966, Moody was in a Catford club called *Mr Smiths* with Eddie and Fraser, when a fight broke out between them and another gang. Fraser was shot in the leg by a man called Dickie Hart who was later found dead. When the police arrived, they arrested everyone standing while the wounded were taken to hospital under guard, to be arrested as soon as they were discharged.

Detective Chief Superintendent Tommy Butler from the Flying Squad took over the inquiry, which resulted in a number of defendants appearing at the Old Bailey. Fraser was charged with the murder of Hart while the others were charged with affray. The police and prosecution shook their heads in disbelief when Moody and two more defendants were found not guilty, although it was no surprise really as jury tampering had reached epidemic proportions.

During the trial, Butler put together enough evidence to ensure the Richardsons would stand before a court to answer for their years of violent torture. Moody had no time to celebrate his freedom as he was arrested again and returned to prison.

In the summer of 1966, at the age of 25, Moody again stood in the dock, this time as one of fifteen defendants accused of torture. There was one man missing that day; George Cornell, another of the Richardsons' enforcers, should have been in the dock, but he had been shot dead by Ron Kray in the infamous murder at the *Blind Beggar* pub. The trial lasted almost three months and resulted in long prison sentences for almost everyone, including criminal supremo Charlie Richardson, who was handed twenty-five years. Unbelievably, Moody was found not guilty and released.

With the Richardsons gone and no one to tell him what to do, Moody floundered. He was in demand as a hitman or punisher, working for London's new crime lords, but he was incapable of the organization required to carry out the contracts. Drinking heavily and increasingly volatile, it took two years for him to be back in the dock when, in October 1958, he and his brother Richard stood trial for murdering 21-year-old William Day, whose party the Moodys had gatecrashed.

Realizing that yet again there had been an epidemic of amnesia sweeping South London juries and it looked likely that Moody would walk free, the prosecuting counsel decided to offer him a reduced charge of manslaughter. Believing he had won again, he pleaded guilty. Each brother received six years, with Richard serving four and Jim serving five.

Once released, his reputation as a hitman soared, although he could never be linked with any murders. His real love, however, was armed robbery and he was recruited by the Thursday gang. Never a leader, but a fearless soldier, he was always first on the list when Charlie 'Top Cat' Knight put his team together for each job.

So when we saw Moody drive out of the caravan park, this was the first time he'd been identified since his release from prison for manslaughter. It later transpired that, following the altercation at the supermarket, he had driven to London and picked up his family. Flush with money, he decided to bring them back to Hamble for a holiday, unaware that he was driving into the open arms of waiting police officers. That is until he stopped at a service station and saw the front page of a local newspaper with the headline about Knightley's police-swerving soggy adventure staring back at him. He drove to the nearest car dealer, sold his Range Rover for silly money, bought a Mini and drove back to London where he disappeared into the London suburbs. It was to be more than a year before Moody reappeared in the most unlikely of circumstances.

At Gatwick Airport on 21 December 1979, passengers were making their way home for Christmas, having just arrived from America. Among them was a drunk, old villain named John Kennedy. His shambolic appearance made it almost inevitable that he would be stopped by customs officers and, as they rummaged through his luggage expecting to find too many cigarettes and far too much duty-free booze, they were amazed but pleasantly surprised to uncover two handguns and boxes of ammunition. Kennedy was arrested and interviewed, but refused to speak to anyone except a detective from Operation Ohio. He said it was regarding Jim Moody. It wasn't long before Detective Inspector Bill Foreman and a colleague arrived, and sat down to listen to Kennedy's story. Kennedy told them that he had been in the States for about eighteen months, on a sabbatical paid for by Moody. Moody had offered him the holiday because he wanted to use Kennedy's flat in Coldharbour Lane, Brixton. Kennedy was only too willing to oblige, especially as it was Moody who was asking and refusal was not an option. He had now run out of money and had phoned Moody asking to be allowed home, only to discover the price for his return was two handguns and their ammunition. Kennedy hoped that passing this information on might help him in his present predicament. It did and he later escaped with a sentence of just eighteen months.

Early the following morning, a team of detectives led by Charlie Snape, and backed up by a team of police marksmen, surrounded the flat in Brixton. Bill made a phone call to the flat and Moody answered. 'Don't do anything silly, Jim,' said Bill. 'The place is surrounded.' Moody said he knew, but he had one request. 'I've got my son with me,' he said. 'Can you give me ten minutes to get ready and then I'll come out? But please make sure my boy is safe.' The police agreed, although later it was discovered Moody and his 15-year-old son spent those minutes hurriedly trying to get rid of evidence. They stuffed so much money down the toilet it blocked the drains for the entire block of flats. (The plumber who cleared the drains were, as you can imagine, heavily supervised). After ten minutes and one further phone call Moody sent out his son. Then he came out and surrendered.

Moody was taken to Brixton Police Station, and interviewed by Charlie and Bill. He was fully aware of his fate and admitted to three robberies, the same ones Knightley had been convicted of. He named no one else and would admit to no more. Moody was one of the few criminals who not only talked about honour among thieves, but actually practised it. He was sent back to Brixton Prison to await trial.

It was a typical frosty morning on 16 December 1980 and the sun was just starting to rise when the air in the streets around Brixton Prison were filled with the wailing of sirens, a warning that there had been an escape, or an attempted escape, from this maximum-security establishment. At that time a number of Irish Republican Army (IRA) prisoners were into the fiftieth day of a hunger strike and among them was a top IRA provisional operative named Gerard Tuite. For months, Tuite and two prisoners who were based in neighbouring cells had planned their escape. His collaborators were an old-time robber called Stan Thompson and a certain Jim Moody.

Thompson's was the only cell with an outside wall and so they worked on making a passage from Tuite's cell to Moody's to Thompson's before breaking out into the exercise yard. Maintenance work was being carried out there and, conveniently for them, scaffolding and scaffold planks were lying around. Quickly, they erected some steps and climbed over the 15-foot fence, dropped down on the other side and were last seen running down Brixton Hill on their way to freedom.

Tuite made his way back to his hometown of Drogheda in southern Ireland where he seemed to live quite openly. He thought he was untouchable, but he was arrested some two years later and made judicial history by becoming the first man to go on trial in an Irish court for terrorist offences on British soil. He was convicted and sentenced to ten years' imprisonment.

Moody's life after his escape from Brixton is far less clear. Fact and fantasy blend together to create a story, which varies depending on which expert is telling it. He certainly went with Tuite to Ireland and joined up with the IRA. He had no religious beliefs and carried out murders for them for monetary reward over a number of years. How many depends on who relays the story, although it could be from three to fifteen.

He returned to England in the late 1980s and was linked to a number of murders over the years. There is evidence to suggest that he was the killer of David Brindle, who died in 1991 in a gangland feud. After this he kept his head down, living quietly in Hackney, east London. On 29 May 1993, having been on the run for almost thirteen years, he was sitting alone at the bar of his local pub, the *Royal Hotel*, when a man came in, ordered and paid for a drink, then calmly turned and shot Moody twice in the back, and then twice in the face. The man then walked out, got into a stolen car and drove off, never to be heard of again. Moody was 52-years-old.

Chapter 9

Back To The Sweeney

A few weeks after our Hamble fiasco, I was called to Charlie's office and told I was being posted back to the Sweeney. Obviously, I had completed my post-car-crash sabbatical and my batteries were now fully recharged. Since leaving three years earlier, the Flying Squad had been reorganized and split into five separate units – one covering Central London and the other four receiving an equal portion of the suburban areas. New bases for each had been established and the squad had been given the responsibility of dealing with every armed robbery in the metropolis. I was to report to Rotherhithe, the office that covered the south east of London and an area that I was most familiar with. It was wonderful. The chief inspector and both detective inspectors were personal friends, and almost all the rest of the team were either friends or people I had worked with over the years. Walking into the office that first day, I was greeted with the usual friendly round of abuse. I was home again.

Life on the squad was never dull. We worked in pairs and with armed robberies at an all-time high, I spent more time with my partner than I did with my wife and family. It was essential that you were paired with someone you liked, trusted and respected, and I was lucky in that respect. Dan and I worked hard, but most importantly we possessed the same gallows humour and we were able to see the funny side of even the most stressful situations.

I have ten books' worth of stories, but one in particular stands out. In one of our quiet times, Dan and I were a bit bored so we decided to have a look at one of Rotherhithe's most notorious criminals. He was a man who had his sticky fingers in most of the criminal activities in the area and if he wasn't involved he certainly knew who was. He ran a small transport yard near the dockland, close to a derelict warehouse, which we decided to use as a vantage point. We climbed the rickety stairs of the building with our radio and binoculars, and settled ourselves on the roof of the building to watch the comings and goings in the yard below. Many observations like this are carried out daily and the chances of them bearing fruit are slim. Yet sometimes lady luck is with you and something happens that starts a chain of events you certainly didn't expect when you got out of bed that morning. About thirty minutes after settling ourselves down and having been quite surprised by the large number of familiar faces wandering about the yard, all became clear when into the yard drove an articulated lorry with HOTPOINT emblazoned on the side. It didn't take a genius to know that a little yard run by a renowned villain was unlikely to have a contract transporting goods for an international company of repute. Getting on the radio we put our team on standby, ready for an afternoon of action.

Within minutes of the lorry arriving, its back doors were thrown open, and out came washing machines, fridges and boxes containing every household appliance made by Hotpoint. They were loaded into cars and vans, and driven away to various destinations around the area, with each vehicle followed by a member of our team and the delivery addresses noted for later attention. An hour later everyone was back in position, and the team hit the yard and arrested everyone who moved and some that didn't. A good afternoon's work: a stolen lorry and load recovered, and all the local stations bulging at the seams with a variety of thieves, handlers and receivers.

The main attraction, however, was the yard's two owners. We wanted to know if they would like to help us with more information in return for a lesser charge. The main man, George, didn't want to know – he would just shut up and take his medicine. But his partner had not long been out from five years in prison and didn't want to go back. We had searched his house and seen the tears in his eyes, as he had hugged his 8-year-old daughter and said goodbye to his wife. Back in the interview room for another round of questions, Dan looked at him and said, 'Think of your 18-year-old daughter,' to which he replied, 'my daughter's only 8.' 'She won't be when you come out,' said Dan. We both watched as the reality of his situation sank in. He was a big man, but as the minutes ticked away he seemed to shrink before our eyes. His shoulders sagged, his head dropped into his hands and he started shaking. We all knew what the next step would be, but it had to come from him. Time stood still as we waited for a minute, maybe two. Then, with a big intake of breath, he sat up straight and said, 'OK. What do you want me to do?'

We told him we wanted something far better than a lorry load of fridges; something like a team of armed robbers. We said that we'd put him on bail and if he came up with something good, then the theft of a lorry load might well become receiving of a cooker. Plead guilty to that and he'd walk away with probation rather than the ten years he was likely to get with his record. He agreed, so it was time to explain the specifics. His contact would be Bill, our detective inspector, and he was to phone in regularly. No meetings would take place until we had something worth meeting about.

A couple of months went by until three weeks before Christmas the call came. Bill and I drove fifteen miles away to a roadside transport café and, dressed in scruffy overalls, we pulled out the *Daily Mirror* and *The Sun*, and joined the informant for a full English breakfast. After a while, Bill and I were in possession of the names, date and location of a planned £1 million armed robbery. He said he'd been asked to take part and we agreed that he should, although the authority for this would have to come from far above our lowly step on the ladder. If we were given the go ahead, it would mean we would be with the robbers every step of the way. Permission was granted, and it was decided he would run from the scene and be allowed to escape.

The more detail he gave the more we wondered if this was put together by Mickey Mouse. The participants were all accomplished robbers and the leader, Billy Tobin, was one of the most prolific in South East London. He'd been arrested a few times, but had always walked away from the Old Bailey sticking two fingers up at the squad. The method, however, was straight out of the movies and we were convinced Tobin would go down for it. The meeting ended, and it was time to go back and face the most cynical people known to man, our fellow detectives who had been informed that we'd see them in an hour.

Bill had the pleasure of standing up in front of everyone and relaying what we'd been told. He explained that we'd been given information that a big job was being planned, which the robbers reckoned could be worth upwards of £1 million in cash. The plan was as follows. Every Friday, the security company Brink's-Mat collect the takings from Croydon Shopping Centre and drive up to Crystal Palace, come down to the roundabout at the bottom of Gipsy Hill and into Alleyn Park, pass Dulwich Prep School, Dulwich College and King's College Hospital, and drive into their main depot in London. The road passing Dulwich Prep is always full of cars parked on both sides of the road and becomes virtually one way. Our robbers intended to order a mobile crane to be delivered to a location in Dulwich at 6.00 am on 17 December. When it is delivered, they will kidnap the driver and tie him up. The crane will be driven to a position opposite or just before Dulwich Prep School and parked. As the Brink's vehicle reaches the roundabout, a skip lorry will pull out in front of it and drive in convoy towards the mobile crane. Once past the crane, the skip lorry will stop so the Brink's vehicle can't get by. The mobile crane will come out from behind it, driven by Tobin, who will crash the overhanging jib of the crane through the rear of the Brink's van to open it up like a sardine can. The team will then jump inside, grab the cash, jump in their vehicles and escape back up towards Crystal Palace. They calculated the whole thing would take no longer than four minutes.

There was a short silence before an eruption of laughter and clapping at the fantasy Bill had just presented. Comments rained thick and fast: 'Who was playing the lead?' 'Never be good box office unless there was crumpet in it.' 'Let's hope the Brink's van wasn't made of kryptonite' and many more. 'How high's the crane Guv?' came a voice from the back. 'We don't really know,' said Bill, 'but thanks for asking Fred 'cause you can find out how high it is when it's down and, while you're at it, find out how high a Brink's van is as well, then we'll know if this is feasible. Any more questions?' For some reason they seemed to have dried up.

Everyone was given a task for that Friday. Some were to follow the Brink's-Mat van discreetly; some were to locate suitable observation points; some were to map every house, garden and building around the proposed site of the crime. Every possible escape route had to be found. Fred came back with his measurements, which had been difficult to obtain as no contact could be made with Brink's-Mat themselves, in case someone was in league with the robbers. To everyone's amazement the plan was possible. Everything checked out, almost to the centimetre.

That Friday the Brink's-Mat van was followed from Croydon. It travelled the exact route given to us by the informant and, as a special bonus, two of the robbers whose names we had been given had also been seen following the van. Suddenly the mood in the office changed. Everyone was on board and wishing the hours away until they could get among the robbers.

One of the biggest problems was that the time of the proposed robbery coincided with leaving time for the pupils at Dulwich Prep School on the last day of term before the Christmas holidays. There was no alternative, but to approach the headmaster and ask for his assistance. He could not have been more helpful and I think it gave him a great thrill to think that he was getting involved in something so alien to his normal life. He said he would inform the parents that, as a special treat to the children, he would give them the rest of the day off immediately after morning assembly. Furthermore, he would remove his car from the garage so that we could use it as a place for us to hide. The school opposite the scene of the proposed crime was to break up the day before and again assistance was asked, and given, for us to use one of the upstairs classrooms as an observation point where video cameras could be set up. Billy Tobin, eat your heart out. This one would be recorded for ever and if it came off, and you get found not guilty again, we might as well all go home and give in.

Every alley, house and garden was looked at to see where we could hide or where there would be a possible escape route for the robbers. We knew which residents worked all day, whose garden had a shed and was protected enough for us to use without permission: not strictly legal, but if it came off, an apology and a bunch of flowers for the lady of the house should help appease any problems. We had to be able to lie in wait out of sight completely because any good gang of robbers would search the area an hour or so before the crime looking for police presence, and this team were good. We knew every blade of grass and planned for every eventuality we could think of, but we were ready for the unexpected because that is what usually happens.

About 4.00 pm on Thursday, Bill got the phone call we had been praying for. Everything was in place; it was a go for tomorrow. 'Don't forget,' said Bill to the informant, 'when it all kicks off, you run down the road on the left-hand pavement and keep your head down.' With a parting shot of, 'Well done and don't lose your bottle,' Bill put down the phone and walked into the office with a huge grin on his face. Every detail was raked over one more time and then it was home for an early night because it was definitely going to be an early morning.

By 6.00 am everyone was in their designated hidey hole. The robbery wouldn't happen until about midday and so the long wait started. Dan and I were in a car with a driver in the headmaster's garage, reading books with blank pages and waiting for a radio message from someone somewhere. The first message came at 7.30 am and was from the detective chief inspector, who was controlling everything from the top-floor classroom in the second of our schools. A calm and measured voice informed us that the crane had arrived and been parked by Tobin. Four and a half hours to go. My adrenaline was in overdrive and my bladder was cursing me for that last cup of coffee. Luckily our driver had thought of everything and produced a gallon can for us to use.

At 10.00 am, children came running out of Dulwich Prep School and into the arms of their parents, full of the joys of Christmas, and blissfully unaware that there were twenty hairy coppers hiding in every crack and crevice. The children's safety was one more tick in the box and one less thing to worry about. Then about 11.15 am it started. The Brink's-Mat vehicle had left Croydon, the skip lorry had just arrived and was parked near the roundabout no more than 300 yards away, and, most importantly, Tobin was pacing up and down near the crane obviously waiting for his lead car to give him the nod that the arrival of the Brink's vehicle was imminent. We stood with the garage door opened slightly, and watched Tobin get in the crane and start it up in a cloud of diesel exhaust.

An earth-shattering crash of grinding metal and a shout over the radio of 'Go! Go! Go!', and we are out and running, trying to take in everything before us in an instant. The left-hand pavement is ours up to the scene and another pair has the same pavement coming the other way. We see them running towards us about 100 yards ahead, but between us is a robber with a gun in his hand running away. We chase and he sprints down the side of Dulwich Prep School, and into the playground at the rear. With adrenaline pumping, we catch up with him and leap on to his back, and we fall in a heap on the ground. We grapple and cuddle, and Dan pulls back his boot to kick the gun from his hands. Looking up, I see the school's entire teaching staff standing at the window one floor up with knives and forks in their hands as, mouths open, they drop turkey and dribble gravy on the canteen floor. It's Christmas dinner for them and we're supplying an impromptu cabaret.

'For Christ's sake don't kick him Dan,' I yell and Dan places his boot on the hand of our villain, pressing so hard that the hand and gun leave an imprint on the tarmac. We handcuff him and start to walk away when the headmaster walks out into the yard. 'Well done lads,' he shouts, followed by, 'I would have kicked him.' It was a magical way of relieving the tension and we chuckled all the way back to the scene.

The sight back on the road was almost surreal. Everything was as we had imagined. The skip lorry was first and the Brink's vehicle had been pushed into it by the mobile crane, which had its jib buried deep inside it. Sacks of money were visible, all ready for the thieves to load up. Unfortunately, for them, they were all lying face down on the road with their guns nearby, being photographed. Tobin looked very glum. He had been taken first while still negotiating the jib of the crane into the sacks of cash. A loaded revolver pointed at him from each side of the vehicle's cab had caused him to switch off the engine and climb down. He had been relieved of his gun and now lay with the rest of his team. On his way to prison at last! A quick count of robbers and we realized we were a couple short, but one was the informant so that was OK.

He had made good his escape, although not exactly as planned. He'd been told to run down the left pavement, but ran down the right and, not knowing who he was, one of the team had hit him over the head with a truncheon causing a nasty wound. Lying on the pavement, he looked up and said, 'I'm the bloody snout.' 'You certainly are,' responded the officer as he picked him up, put him in the back of his car and rushed him to King's College Hospital where his wound was sewn up. As the officer told us later: 'He was the first prisoner I've ever had who was pleased to be stitched up by the police.'

We untied the driver of the crane, who was found in one of the robber's vehicles with a sack over his head and then Charlie appeared with the missing criminal handcuffed to him. They looked as if they'd been playing rugby for a week in the filthiest conditions. Charlie had seen his man run through the front gate of a house and set off in pursuit. One mile later, having gone through four garden fences, across two main roads and a playing field, they had joined together for a tussle on the bank of a *pond* inhabited by Canadian geese. Charlie and his new-found friend Kevin had then slithered and slid through the bird droppings into the green, stagnant, rancid water. To say they both stunk would be an understatement, and they were led to a hosepipe at a nearby house and hosed down. Charlie said thank you and the robber made an official complaint. One man's meat comes to mind. Months later at his trail at the Old Bailey, Kevin told the jury that he was not a robber but a burglar. 'There I was just about to break into a house when I heard crashing and banging from the road,' he said. 'I went to the gate to see what was happening when someone shouted "That's One of them!" They chased me and here I am.' The jury found him not guilty. The following year, Kevin was shot dead whilst carrying out an armed robbery.

With everyone accounted for, it was time to get back to the nick, but then we saw Frank, walking across the school playing field, dragging a man who was kicking and screaming, and refusing to stand. Frank was a detective sergeant and he was our bulldog. Nothing got past him and you just had to point and Frank would fetch. He was large and muscular, and boxed for the Met as a heavyweight (he had a great attack, but no defence: ten fights, lost eleven). As they approached, the screaming got louder and all we could hear was something like, 'Meeeeweeepeeeeee.' The governor bent over him and said, 'For God's sake, calm down. What are you saying?' The man sat up, wiped away the tears, took a deep breath and pointing to a parked Mr Whippy ice cream van, and repeated his scream: 'Me Whippy!'

His ice-cream van had been in front of the school and we were unable to move him on, as it would have compromised our presence. When all hell broke loose he'd made a run for it and Frank had assumed he was a robber. Poor chap was only trying to sell a few 99s. We patted him down and said he could go, and with a hop, skip and a jump he ran up the road shouting his thanks, got in his ice-cream van and drove away with a quick blast of *Popeye The Sailor Man*. Everyone looked at Frank and burst out laughing.

Amazingly, Tobin pleaded not guilty. His defence was that the Sweeney had been after him for years, but he didn't know why. He said that on five previous occasions he had been tried for armed robbery, but the jury could see that he was being persecuted and had let him off. He said this obviously, 'pissed the squad off.' He was simply lying in bed that morning when, at about 6.30 am, the door burst in and 'some of this lot, can't remember which ones exactly', dragged him out of bed, took him to Dulwich and stuck him in the cab of a mobile crane. He didn't know how they'd doctored the film, but it wasn't him driving, it was someone wearing his clothes.

Even more amazingly, some of the jury believed this poor man was the victim of continuous police persecution and thus failed to agree on a verdict. However, a retrial was ordered and this time the jury found him guilty, and he was sentenced to a long term of imprisonment. On his release, Tobin went straight back to robbery, and in 2003 he was sentenced to life imprisonment with a recommendation that he serve a minimum of eleven years. He was 51-years-old.

In the summer of 1981, I was promoted to detective inspector. I wanted it, but dreaded it as it most probably meant sitting behind a desk. I was posted to Brixton in south London and, as this was only a couple of months after the Brixton riots, tension between the community and the police was bubbling just below the surface, and was likely to erupt at any moment. The commander told me that there was a wholesale change of staff and the hope was for a new beginning. I was to take over the Street Offences team, which dealt with every robbery, mugging and fight among the emerging gangs.

The muggings were being carried out mostly by black youths from the poor estates in the area. They couldn't get jobs and a lot of them used drugs as an outlet for their poverty-stricken lives. It was a vicious circle. Drugs cost money and mugging got them money. If we did arrest the perpetrators, we were accused of being racist as most of them were black.

Every arrest was fraught with danger. I never worked out the system, but a stop in a deserted street would turn into a mini riot within a couple of minutes as you were surrounded by a baying mob of twenty or thirty teenagers, both male and female. An arrest had to be made in minutes. The people who suffered most were the victims. This was the time of the 'loony left' Lambeth Council run by 'Red' Ted Knight, which presided over a group of people whose every moment was spent fighting any attempt made by the police to get the law-abiding citizens of Brixton to help. The more you won the more you lost. I had one dealing with Red Ted and that cost me my job at Brixton.

It was almost a year after the riots and the council was undergoing its spending review for the next twelve months. All the council-funded schemes were asked to apply for their funding for the next year and one of these was a workshop to teach the teenagers of employment age the art of Caribbean furniture making. Run by a Rastafarian gentleman, he duly attended the town hall to request the renewal of his £15,000 grant. It was explained to him that the amount included £3,000 towards setting up the project and so this year he would receive only £12,000. He was not overly impressed, and told Knight and his staff that if he didn't get the full amount he would burn down the town hall. He was told £12,000 was the limit and he walked out repeating that threat.

That night a firebomb was thrown through the window of the town hall. A few thousand pounds' worth of damage was caused before the fire brigade could put it out. I was tasked with finding the offender. As I knew he'd made the threats, the furniture maker was our number one suspect so I sent a couple of lads out to arrest him, and, while he was sitting in the cells, I went to see Knight. I told him we had the man in custody and all I needed was a statement outlining the threats the man had made earlier. I was met with a torrent of abuse. He told me it was my job to prove the case, that I was a servant of Lambeth Council and that nobody in his employ would ever make a statement to the police. I explained that unless the man confessed there would be no prosecution without a statement, to which Knight replied: 'Then you will have failed in your duty to protect and serve.'

Back at the police station, I was summoned to the commander's office and told Knight had been on the phone, and wanted me to go and see him again. At the town hall, Knight told me that he wanted police protection as the suspect could find out where he lived and firebomb his house. I said, 'Well it seems we both want something. I need a statement and you need protection. If the man is charged I will oppose bail and then there will be no threat to you.' Knight refused. 'Well,' I continued, 'the man will be released and I guess my advice to you is buy a bloody dog!' By the time I got back to the station it had been decided that perhaps I did not have the diplomatic skills needed for Brixton and a couple of weeks later I found myself as supervisor behind the dreaded desk at Clapham.

Chapter 10

Serial Killer Kieran Kelly

In 1983, I encountered the most bizarre case of my career so far. In the middle of the night, two young probationary constables were patrolling the outer reaches of Clapham Common where they came across a bedraggled tramp named William Boyd. He was over 60-years-old and had been a vagrant for as long as his pickled brain could remember. He was dressed in layers of cast-off clothing and sported an enormous beard, which hung down his front in a tangled mess of white hair. He was well known in the area but apart from the fact that he was always drunk on the cheapest cider or, if times were really bad, methylated spirit, he was little trouble. Police officers would help him to some place out of the way and leave him in seclusion to sleep it off.

This night, however, he was fast asleep in the middle of the common and it was pouring with rain. The two young constables had failed to listen to the older statesmen at the nick who had told them to carry him to Balham's area where he could be left safely in a bus shelter (the only downside being you may well come back a few hours later and find that the Balham officer had moved him back again). These two young men didn't want to leave him out in the rain and had called for a van to take him to the police station, where he would be warm and dry.

Around lunchtime the following day, in the centre of Clapham, police officers responded to a call regarding a robbery. On arrival, they found that an elderly gentleman had been sitting quietly on a bench when two vagrants, Kieran Kelly and Paul McManus had sat down next to him. Within minutes they has stolen the old man's watch and managed to remove his wedding ring from his finger. The two vagrants were arrested and taken to Clapham Police Station. The custody sergeant was horrified to see two more drunken, smelly tramps swaying gently in front of him. He was faced with a dilemma. He had four cells and three vagrants and surely it was better to fumigate one cell than three. Decision made, he placed Kelly and Mcmanus in the same cell as the still snoring Boyd.

At about 5.30 pm I was creeping out the back door in the hope of an early night when a young officer started calling, 'Guvnor! Quick! Down the cells.' I turned and followed him, and there was Boyd on his back with a young sergeant bent over him giving him the kiss of life. I leant over and felt for a pulse, but there wasn't one and I told the officer to stop and helped him up. Boyd was dead. I then noticed that tied tightly around his neck was a pair of long socks knotted together. McManus was screaming at the top of his voice to get him out, but Kelly was sitting calmly on the floor with his shoes beside him and his feet were bare. It didn't take long to discover that Kelly was upset by Boyd's snoring so had taken off his socks, knotted them together and garrotted Boyd. I am proud to relate I solved that murder.

Before talking to Kelly, I sent for his file and was amazed to see that he had only been out of prison for a couple of months, having been released after being found not guilty of murdering a tramp called Toal in a Kennington church yard. The allegation was that the vagrant had been sleeping on a tomb that Kelly felt was his so he'd removed the string he used as a belt and started to strangle him. Apparently another tramp said, 'You might have killed him, Kelly.' Kelly wandered back to the unconscious tramp, gorrotted him again and with a laugh said, 'I fucking have now.' At the Old Bailey some months later, half the witnesses couldn't be found and the others were too drunk to give any credible evidence so consequently Kelly walked free.

Armed with our file, my detective sergeant Andy and I went in to talk to him. His first words were, 'I suppose you want this' and removed the ring he'd stolen that morning from his mouth. There was no dispute about the murder as Kelly confessed eagerly and said, 'The dirty old bastard wouldn't stop snoring. He won't snore anymore now.' With that he burst into a fit of laughter. Wondering if Kelly would now admit to the

Kennington murder, I said, 'The murder in the cells is done and dusted. We thought we would have a chat to you about all the other murders.' Kelly stood up, started prancing about shadow boxing, then he sat down and said, 'I suppose you're talking about Fisher?' 'That would do for starters,' I said, having no idea what he was talking about. I raised my eyes to Andy who left to make a few phone calls. Kelly went on: 'I bet you never knew it was a robbery,' he said. 'No Kelly,' I replied, 'you were far too clever for us on that one.' 'That's why I left £20 in his pocket,' he said. A few minutes later Andy returned and slipped me a piece of paper, which simply said: 'Fisher. Murder. Clapham church yard. Five years ago.' 'What was that all about, Kelly?' I asked. 'Dirty bastard wanted my arse so I stabbed him in the bollocks,' was the reply.

The murder papers later revealed exactly that: £20 had been removed by the medical examiner from Fisher's inside pocket and the wounds inflicted in the course of the murder were exactly as Kelly described. That was the start of days of interviews with Kelly, in which he relayed his life from the day he came to London from Ireland in the company of his best friend Christy Smith in 1953, at the time of the coronation of Queen Elizabeth. His first murder was Smith. His friend had questioned Kelly's sexual preference so Kelly had pushed him under a London Underground train.

There was a couple of years' stability in the early 1960s when Kelly married and started a family, but then his wife's former partner returned and threw Kelly out of the house and on to the street. From then on his life was spent half as a vagrant and half as a prison inmate. He developed a hatred for three types of people: drunks, vagrants and homosexuals, which was ridiculous as he was all three. In the following days he told us of some fifteen murders he had committed over the years. All his victims were members of the vagrant community in south London, but their transient lifestyle made it almost impossible to trace them all. However, we were able to establish that five had died under circumstances that were as Kelly described. He was eventually convicted of two murders, which was enough to ensure he was sent to Broadmoor Hospital for the criminally insane for the remainder of his life. The one murder that he would never admit to was the one in the Kennington church yard, which he had previously been found not guilty of at the Old Bailey. As he told me at the time: 'The court said I didn't do it so I obviously didn't.' Kelly later found his way into *The Guinness Book of Records* as England's most prolific killer, before Dr Harold Shipman took away his title.

A few weeks later I received a phone call that was to lead me on yet another journey. 'Hi Brownie, do you want a job?' It was my old detective chief inspector from the Flying Squad. He was now detective superintendent at Scotland Yard in charge of C11, the criminal intelligence department of the Metropolitan Police. 'Yes please,' I replied. 'You haven't asked me what it is,' he said. 'Is it in Clapham?' I asked. 'No,' he said. 'Then I want it,' I replied. He told me to come and see him in the morning, and I did so, arriving at least an hour early in case he offered the job to someone else and I missed the chance of escaping from Clapham.

He told me that they were running an operation called Kate, the object of which was to monitor the movements of south London's armed robbers. The inspector in charge had been promoted and this had created a vacancy. I thought I had died and gone to heaven but then it got even, better. 'What I really want,' he continued, 'is for you to see if you can find the gold.'

Chapter 11

The Brink's-Mat Robbery

On Saturday, 26 November 1983, the biggest robbery in British history took place when £26 million-worth of gold bullion had been stolen from the Brink's-Mat warehouse at Heathrow Airport. Three of the robbers had been arrested, with two sentenced to twenty years imprisonment and the third being acquitted. The rest of the gang were still at large and there had been no sightings of them or any sign of the gold. The names being linked with the crime were among the highest echelon of London's many armed robbers, but not even they would have the know-how to convert the gold into cash. They would need expert help with that.

When I agreed to work on Operation Kate, I never realized that it would take me around the globe, and uncover a deadly underworld of murder, money laundering and drug smuggling. Maybe the governor had a better ideas as he said to me, 'Find yourself a sergeant who you trust and can work with twenty-four hours a day because that's what it will take.' It didn't take long to come up with a name we both agreed on: an old CID colleague called Tony. It took a couple of weeks for both our transfers to come through and then we sat down to decide how to go about this mammoth task. Although much has been written about the robbery, it would be remiss not to summarize the actual crime.

Brian Robinson, also known as 'The Colonel' because of his ability to plan and execute high-profile robberies, had a sister who was living with a man named Anthony Black. Black was a security guard who worked for Brink's-Mat at their secure warehouse at Heathrow Airport. Over the last few months Robinson and his lieutenant, Micky McAvoy, another top robber whose reputation for violence earned him respect among the criminal fraternity, had befriended Black. They took him fishing on his days off and pumped him with questions about his work while planting ideas in his head of a glorious future life of untold wealth. All he had to do was tell them when the warehouse was full of valuables. Eventually they wore him down.

Every day before he left work, Black would read the manifest to learn what was being held in the vaults and for how long. It was agreed that when the warehouse was stuffed full of riches, he would call Robinson. It was going to be easy. Black was even going to open the door for them.

Robinson assembled his team and made sure they were ready to go at any time. All they wanted now was the phone call. On the evening of 25 November 1983, Black made the call. In the vault was about £3 million in cash as well as diamonds and travellers cheques. It was definitely worth doing and so it was agreed that at 6.30 am the next morning, in they would go.

Unfortunately, Black was not the most reliable of people and the robbers were anxiously waiting for him when he arrived ten minutes late. As agreed, Black went in to join his fellow guards for an early-morning cup of tea, but after a few minutes he said he was desperate for the toilet. Then he went downstairs, opened the door and left it on the latch before heading back upstairs to enjoy his tea. A few minutes later the door burst open and six masked men crashed into the room waving a variety of guns in the guards' faces. The two guards who held the security numbers to the vaults were singled out and the robbers asked for the numbers. When they were not forthcoming quickly enough, McAvoy doused one of them with petrol and stood over him with a lighter. Numbers supplied, the robbers opened the vault. Everything they had been promised was before them and quickly scooped up. But there was more, for, as they turned to leave, one of them noticed a number of crates on the floor and, after breaking one open, they were confronted with rows and rows of neatly-packed gold bars. Each bar was 400 grams of 99.9 per cent pure gold. It took a minute or two before they realized what they had stumbled on. They reversed their old Dormobile van into the loading bay, pulled down the shutters and loaded the boxes. With 2 tons of gold inside, it's a wonder the axles didn't break as they drove away towards south London. They had gone in for £3 million and walked out with £26 million-worth of gold plus the original three in cash as well as diamonds and travellers cheques.

It was pretty obvious to the Flying Squad that there had to be an inside man, and it wasn't long before they established the link between Black and Robinson. As he wasn't a hardened villain and had never been inside a cell, it was inevitable that Black would crack. He named Robinson, McAvoy and another well-known robber, Tony White. He had no knowledge of the other three. C11 had a photograph of six men coming out of a block of flats in south east London taken by a surveillance officer with a telephoto lens just a few weeks before. Robinson, McAvoy and White were identified, alongside two robbers named John Fleming and John 'Little Legs' Lloyd. The sixth man had his back to the camera and couldn't be named. The Flying Squad quickly established the whereabouts of Robinson, McAvoy and White, and arrested them. They were charged and taken to the Old Bailey with Black as the main prosecuting witness. There was little evidence against White, especially as Black could not positively identify him, and he was acquitted, but Robinson and McAvoy were found guilty and sentenced to twenty years. However, Fleming and Lloyd could not be found, and neither could the gold.

Pure gold; you can't spend it, can't sell it, can't do much with it, but look at it and realize you are rich beyond your wildest dreams and yet you haven't got a penny. The squad knew that the gold had to be adulterated (melted and mixed with other metals) and to do that you needed a smelter, a mobile melting pot capable of heating the gold to the necessary temperature. There were only a few smelter manufacturers in the country and two detectives set out to find every one that had been recently ordered or purchased. They also visited every jeweller in London's jewellery quarter, Hatton Garden, and a couple of weeks later they got the information they wanted.

A man with a London accent had made an enquiry about a smelter in a Hatton Garden jewellers and had been referred to a factory in

Evesham, Worcester. The officers phoned the factory and were told that their managing director was at that moment trying to contact them about the order. The officers rushed to the factory and it was agreed that the officers could have an electronic bug concealed in the smelter so it would be traceable at all times. All the officers needed now was the authority of the Home Office (who had to authorize all electronic taps, phones and bugs), which should not be a problem with the evidence the officers could put forward. They also needed the go ahead from the Met's top CID officer, which they also knew would be instantly forthcoming. The officers rushed back to Scotland Yard, thrilled to think that they had made the big break through. They presented their case to the top brass and were amazed when the request to trace the smelter was rejected because it cost too much money. This was almost certainly one of two terrible mistakes that would result in the failure to locate and recover the gold. The officers argued that they only wanted it monitored until it found a home or if it moved. 'Follow it yourselves,' they were told.

On Christmas Eve, only four weeks after the robbery, the smelter was collected from the factory and loaded into the boot of a Rolls-Royce. It was too big and stuck out the back as it set off towards London. The two officers and their squad driver followed it as best they could, making sure they weren't seen. They knew this might be the only chance they had of identifying the person who was going to transform the gold into something saleable. Everything went well until they reached junction three on the M25 motorway. This is the junction for either the A20 to Maidstone or the M20 to Ashford and the Channel Tunnel. The road goes under the motorway, and the entrance to both the A20 and the M20 are very close together, but the officers weren't close enough and didn't know which one the Rolls-Royce had taken. They chose the M20 and they were wrong. They lost the smelter.

They had, however, done a check on the Rolls-Royce and, after driving for a while before accepting they'd lost the car, they headed back to the owner's house to find it sitting on the front drive with the boot firmly shut. They knocked on his door and questioned him about his movements that day. The man was an old-time criminal and was most helpful to the officers. He explained to them that he had been asked by an Indian chap that he had met in a pub to go to the Midlands and collect a crate for him. The Indian gentleman, whose name he didn't know, had offered him £500. He didn't know what was in the crate and he was a bit annoyed at the size of it, as he almost couldn't get it in the boot. He drove down to a lay-by on the A20, met the man, gave him the crate, collected his £500 and came home. He hoped there was nothing illegal in the box, but he was very sorry if there was and he was even sorrier that he could not help the officers with the identity of the Indian chap. The officers thanked him and went home to spend a miserable Christmas wondering what might have been.

There was one more error that would prove costly. The police, and in particular C11, were just starting to join the computer revolution. Yet there was no training and many people who had no idea how to turn on a computer got passwords, which allowed them to access a certain level of information dependent upon their rank. What no one in authority seemed to grasp was that it was no good having a password if you didn't know how to use a computer. In order to access information, it became the norm to get someone who knew what they were doing to use your password and then let you read the text. The whole system was flawed and it would take years to bring it up to anywhere near the standard required.

Just after Christmas a message came in. The real identity was given for a man who had travelled to Jersey under the false name of Mr Swan. He had gone to a jewellers on the island where he had requested to purchase eleven 400-gram bars of pure gold. A further request was that they should be from a company named Johnson Matthey, as he understood they were the most reliable suppliers of fine gold. He was giving an exact description of the stolen gold.

Whoever received that message at Scotland Yard either failed to see its significance or didn't read it at all. The result was that the information stayed in the computer and, to make matters worse, a second message which stated the gold had been collected, paid for and deposited in a safety deposit box at a bank on the island had also been ignored.

Back at Scotland Yard, Tony and I read everything we could on the robbery and the criminals who were believed to have carried it out, and then we read it all again. We chewed over every bit of information, regurgitated it and chewed it again, but nothing was coming forth to create the tiniest spark of inspiration. Tony and I were poles apart in many ways. He was a hunting, shooting, fishing man who owned and trained gun dogs, and put down the pheasants for the local shoot. I was the opposite: if there wasn't a ball involved that you could hit with a racquet or a club I wasn't interested. However, outside interests aside, we were totally in sync and had an almost telepathic thought process. We were obviously fitted with the same model of bullshit antenna. Our humour was similar and based on cynicism, especially in relation to the rubbish we were being fed from the Flying Squad. We both appreciated that it is just as important to know when to say nothing as it is to ask the right questions and we knew when to keep our mouths shut. The trouble was we started this inquiry knowing nothing and a week later we knew lots of things we didn't know before, but we still knew nothing.

There are two main reasons why officers on major inquiries keep secrets. The first is that they don't want information leaking and they're not always sure whom they can trust. The second is far more frustrating; they won't share, they say, because they are so close to solving the crime and they are terrified of the villains escaping before they can hammer in that final nail. Roughly translated this actually means we haven't got a bloody clue. We were sure the second of these excuses applied to the Brink's inquiry.

Over the years there have been many accounts of the Brink's-Mat robbery written by authors, reporters and 'experts', all of whom have had to resort to fiction. They've had to invent informants, circumstances and events in order to explain how the police started to investigate the criminal whose name was to become forever linked to the Brink's-Mat inquiry. There are only two officers who know the real story and neither of them has ever been approached or spoken to by any of the writers.

'Come on Guv, think of something,' said Tony impatiently as we raked over the information again and came up with nothing. 'I can't,' I said. 'The only thing I know at this moment is that I have finished the Kieran Kelly murder report and it needs to go to Brixton to be submitted, so let's do that.' It didn't take long and then we went to the canteen to have a coffee. Sitting there was an old friend, a detective sergeant we had both known for years. He only had a couple of years to go before retiring and what he didn't know about south London criminals wasn't worth knowing. He asked what we were working on and I told him that we had been given the job of finding the gold. 'Who was on the robbery?' he asked. We gave him the names of the arrested and suspected, and he pulled a few faces. Then he said, 'John Lloyd. Little Legs. There's a name from the past. I'll have a bet with you. If Little Legs was on it, his best mate will be in it up to his neck. He wouldn't be a robber, but you won't find a more slippery, double-dyed, clever, devious bastard than this one. He is probably the best middleman I have ever come across, but what a dangerous villain he is. Little Legs isn't clever enough to know what to do with that gold. This guy might not do it all, but I bet he's doing Lloyd's share.'

We knew this was one of those moments to keep quiet, wait and listen. 'Before I give you the name,' he said, 'I will give you a warning, but keep this to yourselves. This man is so well connected; the villains trust him and a number of Old Bill do as well. In my opinion they are all mad.' He picked up a teaspoon, held it out and said, 'If he told me that was a spoon I'd get a second opinion.' He explained that the man had such a cosy relationship with the police he used to wander in and out of his local CID office. 'I don't expect that's changed,' he said. 'Back then he was sharing the pleasures of the CID typist with the top detective, and a Masonic lodge with the detective he gave his information to.' He said he was based outside of London and was the best informant the Regional Crime Squad had ever encountered. 'I suppose you want the name,' he said with a smile. 'The only trouble is I've forgotten it. What usually helps my memory is a really good vindaloo for lunch.'

Over a hastily-arranged lunch of a hot curry, he told us so much about this man and his criminal life that I was starting to get a feeling we might just be on to something. He also confirmed something we did know: Little Legs was living with a gangster's moll called Jean Savage.

Wined and dined to his satisfaction, he ceremoniously pulled out a gold embossed pen, tore a piece of paper from a notebook and, with a flourish, wrote down a name and address, folded it in four and handed it to me. 'I only use this pen on special occasions,' he said, 'and I have a feeling this is one. Good luck and thanks for the Ruby.' Once again, a seemingly random meeting and chance remark had helped me along. I really was a lucky bugger.

Having slept on the information, I picked Tony up early the next morning in our Post Office engineers van, equipped with a ladder on top, and set off for Swanley Police Station to check the collator's records of all the known criminals in the area (as well as any incidents or sightings) when there was no one about. Sure enough the address we had been given was in the system, but the card (for records had yet to be computerized) also had a second address written on it. We set off to the first address, given to us by the loose-tongued detective sergeant. It was a nicely-presented bungalow in Hever Avenue, West Kingsdown, Kent. On the drive was a fairly new vehicle, and we made a note of the reg and went to the nearest phone box to check it out. The car was registered to an address in Falkirk in Scotland in the name of Jean Savage. We had almost certainly found Little Legs. Not bad for an hour's work.

The second address was on the other side of the A20 and as we approached it the area became more rural. Eventually we came to a notice, which said *Sackville House, Residential Home for Retired Clergy*, and opposite was a set of newly-built electronic gates. Behind these, a winding drive around 150 yards long ran into the woods, and we could just see a very large, newly-built, double-storey detached house with wings and garages or stable blocks set in at least ten acres of grounds.

The name on the gate said *Hollywood Cottage*. Down came the ladder and Tony shimmied up the closest telegraph pole. When he came down he said, 'You better look as well.' After a quick scoot up the pole, I knew we had to do a bit more digging about the property and its owner.

Our enquiries created more questions than answers, but it appeared that on this site had stood a tiny, old, two-bedroom cottage, which had been sold to its present occupant. Shortly after he purchased the property he went on holiday to America, and the cottage somehow caught fire and burnt to the ground. His luck changed when the insurance company paid out and he was able to start building his own house. However, we could find no record of planning permission having been granted to build anything and it was unlikely he would have got the green light to build something that size. But, like a phoenix rising from the ashes, this tiny, two-bedroomed cottage had transformed itself into a five-bedroomed, five-bathroom mansion with a 20-metre indoor swimming pool and billiard room. There were garages, sheds and outbuildings, but most interesting of all, underneath the grounds were tunnels and rooms, which had been used as communication centres in the Second World War.

We had a gut feeling that we had stumbled on something, but we needed more time. We could only sit up a telegraph pole for so long without being noticed. 'It's time to pray for divine help,' said Tony and that's exactly what we did. We drove up to the front door of Sackville House and spoke to the vicar in charge of the retirement home for the clergy. Having introduced ourselves, we explained that we needed a room with a view facing the road. Within minutes we were sitting in armchairs in the upstairs lounge, enjoying a cup of tea and a plate of custard creams, with a perfect view of the entrance to Hollywood Cottage.

Within an hour, a Ford Cortina had pulled up to the gates, entered the code into the keypad, and driven up to the house and out of view behind the trees. A quick phone call and we were told the vehicle was stolen. About an hour later the Cortina came out. The good thing about these gates was that the car had to stop and wait for them to open, by which time we'd got a good view of the driver through our binoculars. Ten minutes

40 DIE, 75 HURT IN RAIL CRASH

Crowded coaches jump track near Lewisham disaster spot

By Malcolm Stuart, Michael Rhind, Robin Robinson and Leslie Toulson

FORTY PEOPLE were killed last night when a crowded diesel-electric train crashed at Hither Green, South East London. Seventy five passengers were injured.

Ten of the 7.43 Hastings-Charing Cross

Hither Green rail disaster, 5 November 1967.

Reg and Ron Kray (l–r) with older brother Charlie.

Lisa Prescott, Mitchell's hired companion.

Frank 'The Mad Axeman' Mitchell.

Receiving the Queen's Commendation for Brave Conduct.

Jim Moody, robber, hard man and hired killer.

Flying Squad ambush £1 million gun raiders

By TIM MILES

The security van jammed between lorry and mobile crane . . . and weapons left by the raiders in their van

A GANG of shotgun raiders were ambushed by the Flying Squad yesterday as they were battering open a security van containing nearly £1 million with a mobile crane.

Three shots were fired at the bandits as they attempted to escape from the scene outside Dulwich College Preparatory School in South-East London.

One of the men, wielding a sawn-off shotgun, fell to the ground believing he had been hit, but the police bullet had intentionally gone wide of the mark.

Teachers and domestic staff enjoying their traditional end-of-term Christmas lunch watched in amazement as another of the gang was pursued by detectives across the back garden and brought down with a tackle.

Last night six men were being questioned at East Dulwich police station.

Detectives had known for two weeks that a major robbery was being planned. By Monday, they knew precisely when and where it was to take place.

Yesterday a team of 30 officers had been in hiding since the early hours of the morning, adopting a number of disguises to avoid arousing suspicion.

Shortly after 1 p.m. a Brinks-Mat security van, en route to the City with its cargo of cash collected from banks in the Croydon area of Surrey, turned into Alleyn Park, Dulwich.

Suddenly, a lorry swung out in front of the armoured van, forcing it to brake sharply.

Simultaneously a truck equipped with a crane jib rammed into the back, splicing open the metal-plated security doors like a giant tin-opener.

Two transit vans carrying other members of the hold-up gang surrounded the three-man security crew.

The police opened fire when it was thought that a raider was preparing to take aim. But as one officer put it : 'They had no real chance to use their guns. We were on them before they got to the money. It was all over in seconds.'

Newspaper report on the Dulwich robbery.

The Brink's-Mat vehicle with the crane rammed in the back.

Leader of the Dulwich robbery gang, Billy Tobin.

Serial killer Kieran Kelly.

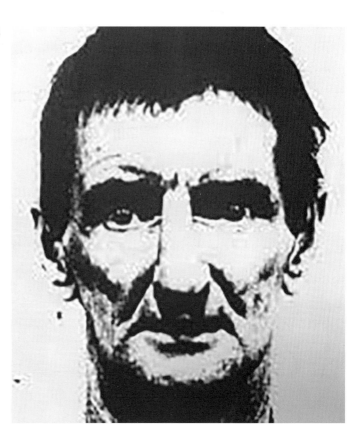

Kenneth Noye's house, Hollywood Cottage.

Anthony Black, the inside man in the Brink's-Mat gold bullion robbery.

Brian Reader. Noyes Lieutenant and courier of the Brinks–Mat Gold.

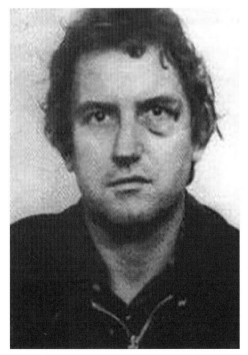

Kenneth Noye immediately after his arrest for the murder of police officer John Fordham.

Kathy Meacock with dogs, Brinks and Mat.

MURDER OF A TOP SPY COP

Hero knifed in search at mansion

SCOTLAND YARD'S top undercover man has been murdered.

John Fordham, a 45-year-old detective constable, was stabbed when he went to search a £250,000 mansion in Kent at the weekend.

Father of three Fordham was on a lone mission for C11, the Criminal Intelligence Branch.

He was knifed in the mansion's eight - acre grounds — possibly after disturbing four Rottweiler guard dogs.

DANGEROUS

Fordham, who had been trained in SAS-style skills by the Army, was the Yard's most-expert shadow. But he always refused promotion, preferring to remain a constable.

Last night a Yard chief said: "John was brilliant at keeping observation under cover. He was the

By GEORGE HOLLINGBERY

best-trained surveillance officer in the country."

Fordham's highly dangerous work, often in disguise, involved trailing top gangsters and unearthing information about criminal operations.

He had been commended four times—for brilliant work on two murder cases, a manslaughter inquiry and a blackmail investigation.

Last night two men and a woman were being quizzed by police about the ace detective's death.

Fordham was attached after he had gone to the

Continued on Page Two

Victim . . . undercover cop John Fordham

Newspaper report on John Fordham's murder.

KENNETH NOYE
GORDON PARRY
BRIAN PERRY
MICHAEL RELTON
JOHN ELCOMBE
BRIAN READER
JEAN SAVAGE
PATRICK CLARKE
JOHN "GOLDFINGER" PALMER
GARTH CHAPPELL
MICHAEL LAWSON
KATHLEEN McAVOY
TERENCE PATCH

All were convicted or had to repay millions to insurance investigators in civil claims.

UK detective to head drug squad

By Rick Bruner

To battle what is seen as a "growing drug problem" in the BVI, government has turned to the United Kingdom for expert help to lead local forces.

Ian Brown, a senior detective on the London Metropolitan Police force, will arrive here next Sunday, to take command of the newly formed drug unit of this police force.

Commissioner of Police Ronald Thompson said the need for a local drug unit and an expert commander was recognized last year. Drug trafficking, he said, is becoming an increasing problem here as enforcement through other routes strengthens. Local use of drugs is also on the rise as a result of the trafficking, said the commissioner, as the transporter often "pay off in kind."

Most of the drugs being

continued on page 13

My appointment to the British Virgin Islands.

The Island Sun

SUN ENTERPRISES (BVI) LTD PUBLISHERS

OVER 400 KILOS OF COCAINE SEIZED AT BEEF ISLAND AIRPORT

Swift action by immigration, police and customs officers leads to the arrest of two Colombians

By Vernon Pickering

A combined effort by immigration, police, and customs officers deployed at Beef Island has resulted in the largest seizure of narcotics ever made in the territory.

When two Colombians descended from a Piper plane which had landed at Beef Island Airport, 7:45 pm on Sunday (May 22nd) they were confronted with routine formalities -- or so they thought.

Instead, the immigration officer, who was the first to check them out, became very suspicious. This was immediately confirmed by customs and police officers on duty at the local airport facility.

Swift action by immigration, customs, and police officers led to the search of the Piper which was laden with some 417 kilos of cocaine.

Assistant Superintendent of Police Mr. Ian Brown said the two Colombians had flown directly from Colombia to Beef Island.

British Virgin Islands Magistrate J. A. Patrick Emmanuel Tuesday afternoon denied bail to the two Colombians arrested here Sunday after their drug-laden twin-engine aircraft landed at Beef Island

Continued on page 23

Report in The Island Sun.

The BVI drug squad (l-r) Detective Sergeant Balti, me, my wife Beth, Detective Constable Devonish, Detective Station Sergeant Forbes, Detective Constable Martin (kneeling).

500 kilos of pure cocaine with a street value of $400 million.

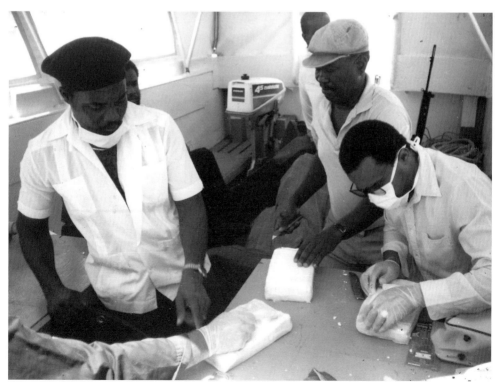

Opening the cocaine before throwing it in the sea.

One million dollars' worth of cocaine slips through my fingers.

Returning the cocaine to nature.

Me, higher than a kite.

Fish feeding frenzy.

The flying squad swoop on a drug-filled dinner.

Coolers containing 300 kilos of cocaine dropped in the sea near Princess Diana.

Diana, oblivious to the drug busts nearby. (*Getty Images*)

On top of the world. Some of the 6 tons of cannabis siezed.

The New Police Launch, Ursula.

Me with the police plane, which had been seized from Columbian drug dealers.

later, a Range Rover came down the drive from Hollywood Cottage and we got our first perfect view of the house's owner, Mr Kenneth Noye, who we recognized from the collator's records. We needed help.

Back at Scotland Yard we sat down with our boss. We needed a surveillance team, a big one, but we were a non-operational unit. If this had anything to do with the Brink's–Mat robbery, it was the Flying Squad's inquiry. However, we had no evidence of anything, just a churning gut feeling and we needed another day of observations. So a surveillance team of cars, vans, motorbikes, walkers and riders were briefed and sent to hide away somewhere near West Kingsdown (but to avoid Hever Avenue). Then we, and other officers, settled back into the comfort of the front room of Sackville House. It was our turn to supply the custard creams.

Two hours passed and then the Ford Cortina arrived, exactly the same time as the day before, entered through the gates, went up the drive and returned half an hour later to pose for a picture taken with a telephoto lens. The Cortina was tailed all the way to Hatton Garden. The driver parked and went to the nearest telephone box to make a call. Little did he realize that the smelly old vagrant leaning against the box was noting the number he dialled. After returning to his car, he went into a café and sat at the window drinking coffee. Within minutes a white Mercedes came down the street and reversed into a space behind the Cortina. With the cars parked boot to boot, the new man entered the café, and the two men sat drinking coffee and chatting. Another five minutes and both men came out, opened both car boots, and the second man leaned in to the Cortina and came out with a Gladstone bag, which was obviously heavy, as he needed two hands to lift it. This was transferred to the Mercedes, and the men got in their respective cars and drove away in opposite directions.

The surveillance team split so it could follow both cars. About 100 yards later, just by chance, a lorry pulled out in front of the vehicle following the Mercedes. Blocked with no way to pass, the tail was aborted and the Cortina became the target. It was followed to Eltham where the driver let himself into a house with a key.

Had we watched a handover of gold? We certainly thought so, especially when it was confirmed that the driver of the Mercedes was a dodgy Hatton Garden jeweller. When photographs of the day's work were developed, the identity of our Cortina driver was confirmed as Brian Reader, who was wearing the most horrendous, obvious wig that had ever been conceived. Reader at that time was in an open prison, where he was allowed out daily to work his way towards his release as a fully-reformed member of society. I'm not quite sure he had managed to find an honest and trustworthy occupation in his quest for redemption.

It was time to present our findings to our governor. We couldn't go any further without authority and so a meeting was arranged with Scotland Yard's top brass, who discussed the onward plan. Tony and I sat in the corner, on the one hand proud and elated that we had helped to advance the inquiry, and yet saddened that we'd lost our freedom, as we'd no longer be able to make decisions without a senior officer's authority.

Suddenly, the manpower required to investigate the Brink's-Mat robbery multiplied. Within a couple of hours, a detective chief superintendent was required to head the investigation. A complete floor of Tintagel House, the Met's office near Vauxhall Bridge on the south bank of the Thames, was cleared and, in a blink of an eye, transformed into the new headquarters of the Brink's-Mat inquiry. A whole new structure was created and electronic surveillance previously denied was readily available. Tony and I joined forces with Fred, a detective sergeant from the Flying Squad who had been on the inquiry since day one and knew every detail. We got our own office and became the intelligence cell, and, as such, we were to read and disseminate all incoming information.

As an aside, Vauxhall was to be the scene of the most embarrassing moment of my police career. One day, on my way to work, I stopped at a bank near Tintagel House to withdraw some cash. I joined the shortest queue before realizing the queue to my left was moving far quicker, so I switched, collected my cash and went to the office. Twenty minutes later my phone rang. 'Did you get your cash OK from the bank this morning?' asked my friend, who was in the Flying Squad. Surprised, I said, 'I didn't see you there,' to which he responded: 'You didn't see the black woman with a gun holding up the cashier next to you either did you?' This story always gets slipped into conversation when in the company of that particular friend.

Another surveillance operation was set up to follow Reader and the Cortina, and that very first night we placed a bug under his car. He had parked his car outside his house under a streetlight and someone had to act as lookout while our technical officer crawled under the car. I phoned my daughter, Mandy, who had followed me into the profession (primarily because she wanted some excitement in her life and because I told her not to) and was a police constable at Croydon. I then gave her some unusual instructions. We met a mile away from Reader's house and at 1.30 am we parked opposite his home, and Mandy and I simulated a heavy petting session while talking to the technical officer as he lay on his back under the car. I don't think she's ever told anyone she spent a couple of hours pretending to snog her dad on the Brink's-Mat inquiry.

The following day the signal from the Cortina was being picked up loud and clear, but it was a couple of days before it made its way back to Hollywood Cottage. There was no need to have visual contact with the target vehicle unless it stopped, and then the foot surveillance officers would take over. Once again, Reader left the mansion and drove to Hatton Garden, sat in the same café, used the same phone box, rang the same number and the same Mercedes car pulled up, but this time there were two men. They had the same exchange at the boot of the Cortina, but now it was two Gladstone bags, one for each man.

There was no way the Merc was being lost this time. It was followed into central London until it parked, and the two men got out carrying the bags and walked straight into Paddington Railway Station. This wasn't the end; it was just the beginning. They went to the ticket booth and bought two returns for Swindon, observed by one of our walkers. Immediately the cars and vans were off and running. It was only fifteen minutes before the train departed and although they didn't have much chance of getting to Swindon before the train, they had to try. The motorbikes were already cutting through the London traffic towards the M4 and it was decided that a number of the officers would get on the train as well. It was the middle of the day and the train was empty. As someone said later, there were fifty four people on that train, a driver, a guard, two villains and fifty coppers.

When the train pulled into Swindon, only the two crooks disembarked and it was decided that, rather than all the police get off with them, there would be a 'husband and wife' with their pull-along case containing the radio, a young man, an old man, and one frumpy old lady hobbling along and leaning heavily on her walking stick; all police officers hiding in plain sight. Unfortunately, the cars, vans and bikes hadn't caught up with the train and the team were now stranded at Swindon Railway Station. However, there was no one to meet the bad guys either. They had looked at the only taxi before shaking hands and separating, leaving the station in opposite directions. They were obviously on high alert looking for a tail, and were kept in sight as they did a complete circuit of the station and met up again.

By this time the motorbikes were here and one car was nearby. A black Jaguar drove into the car park, stopped next to the men, and they jumped into the back and headed off towards Bristol. The bikes followed while more cars arrived to pick up our disguised team of walkers. The car was followed to Bedminster, just outside Bristol, and there, right in front of them, was the white gable end of a building and emblazoned on the side, in red letters over a metre high, was the word 'GOLD'. Underneath this was 'SCADLYNN LTD' and beneath that 'BEST PRICES PAID' with an arrow pointing to a shop front. The three men parked outside and entered the building.

In that moment we knew who was turning the gold into cash. We had found one end of the rainbow, but rainbows have two ends and back in London someone was controlling the other. Noye was at least one step removed from the original bullion. We had to find out where he got it from. Did he collect it or was it delivered?

That night, heads locked together on the top floors of Scotland Yard. It was decided that we needed to get surveillance officers in the woods, close to Noye's back door, when the Cortina came in. We could then see if Noye had the gold somewhere in his grounds or in his car. If it was established that he went out to collect the gold then, when all was quiet in the middle of the night, his car would have to be bugged. The Met's SAS-trained surveillance officers were chosen for this task and, on the evening of 26 January 1985, Neil Murphy and John Fordham climbed over the side fence of Noye's property and crept quietly into the woods near the kitchen door.

It was dark and dismal when the Cortina arrived at Hollywood Cottage and drove up to the house. The two men watched as Noye and Reader chatted away outside the kitchen and then, for no apparent reason, Noye opened the kitchen door and released two Rottweiler dogs, who started barking loudly and headed towards the woods. Obviously disturbed, Noye went into the kitchen and reappeared with a torch in one hand and a kitchen knife in the other, and headed for the woods. Worried they were going to be discovered, Neil said, 'Let's go John' and ran for the fence. As he scrambled over, he looked back expecting John to be with him, but he wasn't and he could see a commotion in the woods. He raised the alarm over the radio and then he saw John running towards the front gate, but before he could reach it, he collapsed. He had received multiple stab wounds, which tragically ended his life.

Officers poured through the gates, and arrested Noye and his wife Brenda. Reader had run and was arrested about an hour later on the A20 trying to hitch a lift back to London. The car that stopped was a plain-clothes police car, which was only too happy to give him a ride. It was inevitable that the press would print their version of events the following day and so it became necessary to arrest everyone already identified as being involved in the Brink's-Mat money-laundering operation in Bristol. Search warrants were obtained for every known address and at 5.30 am the following morning, houses and businesses were raided by the police, and arrests were made. After a final tally there were three notable absentees. Two of the men believed to be members of the original robbery team – John 'Little Legs' Lloyd and John Fleming – had not been found and, at the Bristol end, one of the directors of Scadlynn, John Palmer, had gone with his wife to Tenerife for a fortnight's holiday. It proved to be the longest two weeks in history.

The search of Palmer's house, which was called *Battlefields*, revealed a shed in the garden containing a smelter, which was capable of melting and mixing metals, including gold. However, Palmer was alerted by his associates and, faced with the choice of a prison cell or the good life in the sun, he decided to extend his holiday. At that time there was no extradition treaty with Spain and Palmer was free as long as he stayed in Tenerife. Not only would he escape justice, but he would also be able to expand his vast fortune.

Major criminals know that to stay at the top of your profession you have to diversify. In those days, many British pensioners dreamed of buying a home in the sun and, because of the limited funds available to them, the timeshare market was booming. With timeshare you could buy a villa for just one week of the year. Unfortunately, some of these holidaymakers were sheep ready for fleecing and Palmer was able to take the wool from their backs. He ran a timeshare enterprise with a mixture of intimidation and violence. He swindled the British public out of millions of pounds and left them with no hope of either occupying their holiday homes or getting their money back.

Born in Birmingham in 1950, Palmer spent his early life working as a roofer and scrap dealer, and other jobs that earned him cash in hand. By the late 1970s, he was living in Bristol and had become partners with Garth Chappell. These two had a number of businesses together, including a second-hand car site and a business selling used car parts. They then opened a furniture shop in Bedminster and were found guilty of obtaining credit by fraud relating to that business, and received suspended sentences. The pair then opened a scrap gold business named Scadlynn Ltd in the rooms above their furniture shop.

By 1981, the business had a turnover of £6 million, but so many criminals are incapable of running a straight business, even when they have a good thing going as Palmer and Chappell obviously had. So, with the help of one of the best receivers of stolen jewellery the Met Police had ever had, they put together a scheme to avoid paying VAT, thus increasing the profits by the-then VAT rate of 17.5 per cent. It is widely believed that it was this old fence who introduced them to Noye and his operation.

By 1986, Palmer was living in Tenerife with an estimated fortune of £300 million, which meant he had reached the giddy heights of 105 on *The Sunday Times Rich List*, a position he shared with the Queen. But then his passport expired and he was ordered to leave Tenerife. He flew to Brazil, perhaps because he hoped to emulate Ronnie Biggs, who had escaped justice there for sixteen years and would remain for another fifteen. This time the Brazilian authorities were forewarned of Palmer's arrival and did not want the diplomatic problems that would appear if they allowed him to enter the country, so he was put on a flight to London.

At Heathrow, Palmer received a warm welcome from the Brink's-Mat squad, who were looking forward to his arrest and the long prison sentence that would surely be imposed on him when the Old Bailey jury returned their guilty verdict. However, the only certainty in British justice is that when it comes to jury verdicts, there are no certainties. Palmer's partner Chappell had previously been convicted for his part in the gold bullion heist and had been sentenced to ten years. Thus, it was no surprise when he stood in the witness box and swore on oath that Palmer was not a director of Scadlynn at the time of these offences, and therefore had no knowledge of the gold-bullion dealings. Despite the fact that Palmer admitted melting the gold bars in his garden smelter, the jury chose to believe him when he stated that he did not know the ingots were stolen. Despite overwhelming evidence being presented by the prosecution counsel, the police officers involved were lost for words when Palmer was found not guilty in 1987.

Returning to his timeshare con in Tenerife, he was able to steal an estimated £30 million by means of fraud, intimidation and violence from an estimated 20,000 people from around the world. It was fourteen years before he would stand trial at the Old Bailey again, for the largest timeshare fraud on record. Demonstrating his egotistical belief that he was better than the law, he sacked his legal team and chose to represent himself, but was found guilty and sentenced to eight years in prison. None of his victims received a penny back.

Back in Bedminster, the investigation into Scadlynn's accounts was bearing fruit, but unfortunately the fruit was lemon and unbelievably bitter: the more that was uncovered, the worse it got.

Scadlynn had been banking at the Bedminster branch of Barclays Bank for a number of years and their accounts were consistent with a small company just about ticking over, until a few weeks after the largest gold-bullion robbery in British history when this small scrap gold company started to deposit and withdraw large amounts of money. Within a month the company was withdrawing up to £1 million a day, collecting it in anything from cardboard boxes to black bin liners. Concerned by this sudden upturn in business, branch manager Angus Leng reported it to his Bristol head office. Incredibly, their response was to allocate him two extra staff to assist in the handling of the Scadlynn account. Over £10 million would be laundered through that account and, when interviewed for a television programme at a later date, Leng explained that bank customers were entitled to confidentiality and without a court order there was nothing he could do.

Even more incredibly, in order to speed things along for Scadlynn, which was having a torrid time lugging so much money around in bin bags, head office requested from the Bank of England that a complete run of fifty pound notes be made available for them. The Bank of England agreed and every fifty pound note starting A24 made its way to Bedminster and Scadlynn. While this was either incredibly naïve or stupid beyond belief by Barclays, it turned out to be fortuitous to the investigation as anyone found in possession of notes in that sequence could only have got them from the money allocated to Scadlynn and were then guilty of receiving proceeds from the robbery.

If Barclays Bank had been an unwitting accomplice to the crime, so was the Sheffield Assay Office. All scrap gold has to be sent through assay offices in order to test its purity before it can be purchased on the open market. These offices must surely be the first places to notice an increase in the amount of gold coming through the doors. At this point, more than 2 tons of stolen gold was floating about, and the only way it could be sold and legitimized was to have it pass through an assay office. Once it left the office it was free to be sold to the highest bidder and, ironically, the highest bidder for much of the stolen gold was Johnson Matthey, the very company who had owned it when it was first deposited into the Brink's-Mat vaults at Heathrow Airport.

Shirley Carson was the assay master dealing with the Scadlynn account at that time and she is on record in a television interview telling her story, which again is quite remarkable. She said they did think it was a bit strange as the gold was very crudely smelted, but when they asked Scadlynn if they could do the smelting, they said they were doing it themselves. 'One time there was a piece of gold that had not melted properly, and we tested that and found it was pure gold,' she said. 'We nicknamed that piece "the skull" as it looked like a skull. We did think things, but then when customers register with us everything is confidential, so being confidential, nothing was ever said about it.'

The loss adjusters weren't so forgiving and made a civil claim, suing Barclays Bank for more than £24 million for failure in its duty to question the activities of Scadlynn. The matter never went to court, so one must assume it was resolved between the parties. Money aside, it is hard to accept that an anonymous tip off from either company may well have saved John Fordham's life.

John's murder, and the subsequent raids and arrests, changed the Brink's-Mat inquiry overnight. All the people who had their fingers in the pot of gold were now aware that the police knew more than they previously thought. Little Legs made good his escape, although later he found himself on America's most wanted list. The other suspect,

Fleming, had vanished and we were still no nearer to finding who was holding the remains of the gold.

More help was needed so Detective Chief Superintendent Brian Boyce, who was in charge of the investigation, was presented with a new deputy chosen for him by senior officers. Detective Superintendent Tony Lundy was a controversial figure; he had been commended by commissioners and judges more times than any other, as well as being investigated by the police and the press. He'd been suspended and reinstated, sent back to uniform and brought back to CID. One thing is certain, he was a survivor and probably the best detective I ever worked with. Lundy and Boyce were chalk and cheese, and not fond of each other. They also had different ways of working. It soon became apparent that you were either Lundy or Boyce: you couldn't be on both sides.

As with every inquiry, one day you're chasing your tail wondering where to go for the next lead and then overnight you still don't know which way to go because so many leads have appeared, and you have to decide which one to tackle first. In order to tell the story in the easiest way, I'll deal with the important developments, but not necessarily in the order in which they occurred.

Chapter 12

Silence Is Golden

For months, two senior officers had been having covert meetings in prison with both Micky McAvoy and Brian 'The Colonel' Robinson in the hope that they could come to an agreement, which would lead to a possible reduction in their sentences in return for the gold. The stumbling block was that as they were in prison, they had no control over whoever they had entrusted with the gold. McAvoy had a complicated love life as he was married to Jacqueline McAvoy, but was completely besotted with a woman by the name of Kathleen 'Kathy' Meacock, a gangster's moll who had done the rounds of the robber fraternity. He was in the process of divorcing Jacqueline and hoping to set up home with Kathy on his release from prison (he did later marry her in Leicester Prison), and Kathy had become his trusted lieutenant, and he used her to convey messages and instructions to the outside world.

Mail from McAvoy was being monitored and one letter to Kathy told her not to trust Brian Perry. Perry was a well-known south-east London criminal and was thought to be a good friend of the McAvoys. However, it transpired that Perry had been tasked by McAvoy with looking after the interests of both his wife Jacqueline and Kathy. Perry took this task to heart and was soon making sure that Jacqueline was safe at all times, and to ensure this happened he occupied her bed each night. McAvoy's fears were proved accurate when Kathy visited Perry in his Peckham minicab office, for there on the wall was a freshly-painted framed sign which said: 'Remember the golden rule. Whoever has the GOLD makes the RULES.'

The officers who were meeting with McAvoy were wasting their time talking to a man that no longer held any authority on matters relating to the gold. This was confirmed when they received a phone call from Tony White (the robber who was acquitted when tried with McAvoy and Robinson) to arrange a meeting. White, who arrived with Perry, told the officers that, 'McAvoy might think he's in control but he ain't.' He then said it was pointless trying to get the gold back as it was no longer in its original state. They were informed that McAvoy's gold had disappeared and now existed as cash, the location of which McAvoy had no idea. It soon became apparent that Perry was the senior man. It was time to turn the spotlight away from McAvoy and focus it elsewhere.

Enquiries revealed that both Jacqueline and Kathy had moved to new homes since the robbery. Kathy lived in Turpington Farm, an eighteenth-century, six-bedroomed farmhouse set in substantial grounds in Bickley, south London. For a woman with no visible means of support, this was one hell of a step up in the world from her previous home: a run-down council flat just off the Old Kent Road. Jacqueline had also left her flat in Herne Hill, south London, and now resided in a fine detached house in Bickley, just a stone's throw away from Kathy. Perry himself had also gone up in the world, leaving his modest home in Peckham for a lovely house with tennis court and pool in two acres of grounds in Biggin Hill, Kent.

The property records were checked to find out where the money came from to buy these properties and a new player emerged, and an unlikely one at that. All the transactions had been handled by Michael Relton, a respected solicitor, well known for representing criminals. He was also a partner in a property company called Selective Estates, which had recently acquired large holdings in the London Docklands development as well as further property in Spain. The other partners in the company were Perry and a man called Gordon Parry. It looked like the gold was being converted into prime real estate.

Parry and Perry (and yes, this did sometimes lead to confusion) had met through their children as Parry's son and Perry's daughter were living together (or was it the other way round?). Parry was an old-time fraudster, always on the lookout for a way to make money, and he soon realized that Perry was awash with money and not the most astute of men. Perry needed guidance with future investments and Parry was just the man to supply the expertise. Among the schemes conjured up by Parry and Relton to assist Perry in his fledgling money-laundering career was the purchase of land in the London Docklands development. The land was bought at rock-bottom prices; they were all legitimate deals, but paid for with money raised from the sale of the stolen gold.

Parry had also being doing well since the robbery, having bought a beautiful old country house named Crockham House near Westerham in Kent. Set in landscaped grounds and not far from Chartwell, Winston Churchill's old home, it had been extensively renovated since Parry had bought it, and now boasted gold taps in the kitchen and bathrooms.

It was decided to bring Parry, Perry and Relton in for a chat. Perry came without a struggle and Relton was found, but when Parry was approached at a warehouse complex in south London, he managed to drive off with an officer hanging from his bonnet. It would be more than two years before he was arrested in Spain and brought back to face trial at the Old Bailey.

Criminals have no fear of being confined to a small police cell and can endure endless hours of police interrogation; the only thing that bothers them is the lack of TV. A solicitor, however, who had only entered a cell to consult with a client, and was buoyed with the knowledge that he was only there for a few minutes and just had to knock on the door to leave, is a different matter. Relton was shaking like a leaf long before he was led down the dark corridor to his cell. The slamming of a heavy steel door is a sound like no other, and one glance at the wooden bunk and toilet in the corner of this 10ft by 6ft windowless dungeon, with one dim light bulb and graffiti everywhere you look, was enough to start the palpitations.

After leaving him to stew for a few hours, the officers took him to an interview room for questioning. Relton was quick to admit his part in the money laundering. After a couple of hours of painstakingly recording each question and answer, it became apparent that this could take days or even weeks. Much to the officers' surprise, Relton told them the operation was far too complex to go into in this way, and wouldn't it be better if he wrote his own statement and drew some flow charts explaining where the money had come from, where it went and the names of the companies now holding the funds?

It took days for him to complete the picture of the transactions he had organized with Perry and Parry, as well as the accounts he'd opened for Noye, Little Legs, Jean Savage, a friend of Savage's called Patrick Clark and many more. There were accounts in Switzerland, Lichtenstein, the Cayman Islands and Panama, to name just a few. The thought, preparation and methods used by Relton and Parry made this one of the cleverest, and complex frauds the officers had seen and it would never have been uncovered without Relton's help. All that remained was for him to throw himself on the mercy of the court, plead guilty and promise to help the police in any way he could. He would get a sentence of five or six years and, as he was no risk to society, he would be transferred to a relaxed prison to serve his time.

Whatever prompted Relton to go to court and plead not guilty only he knows, but, to add insult to stupidity, his defence was that the detectives had made it all up and fabricated the evidence against him. Relton had forgotten that all the evidence against him was written in his own handwriting. The jury found him guilty and an unimpressed judge sentenced him to twelve years imprisonment.

In early 1993, Perry and Parry were both found guilty at the Old Bailey. This was a retrial as they had managed to dupe the first jury into being unable to reach a verdict. They were both sentenced to eleven years (although Perry had already served two years so he received nine). Both men were stripped of their traceable assets, including their houses.

Kathy Meacock was also arrested and questioned about how she could afford her wonderful new house. When the officers arrived at her door they were greeted by two large Rottweiler dogs. Bending down to pat the dog, one of the officers noticed its name tag: 'Brinks'. It was no surprise to find the other was 'Mat'. It was later discovered even the tortoise at the bottom of the garden had been given the name 'Ingot'. This shows a wonderful sense of gangster humour and a total contempt for authority.

Jean Savage was known as 'the bag lady' as it was her job to go from bank to bank around south east London with large sums of money in a plastic carrier bag, depositing it in various dodgy accounts. She had been doing this for months and had managed to bank millions of pounds on the gang's behalf. A few days after police realized the significance of the A24 fifty-pound notes. Jean was on a banking mission. Her task for the day was to deposit £300,000 in crisp notes at a bank in Croydon. Savage had a daughter who lived in Chislehurst, Kent, and as this was halfway between her home in West Kingsdown and Croydon, she decided to pop in for a coffee. Strolling down the high street, she managed to drop £12,500 on the pavement. Unaware of her mistake, she had a lovely visit with her daughter and continued to Croydon.

The money was emptied on to the counter and the cashier counted out £287,500. Savage panicked, knowing that the gang would assume she'd stolen the difference. After searching the car, she retraced her steps to Chislehurst and arrived at Chislehurst Police Station. She asked the desk sergeant if anyone had handed in her lost cash. The sergeant smiled and said, 'Well Madam, there is good news and bad news. The good news is that an honest citizen found it and handed it in. The bad news is that a dishonest citizen lost it.' Coming around the desk and cautioning her at the same time, he slapped a pair of handcuffs on her wrists and muttered 'A24'. Savage was later sentenced to five years and would serve most of that the hard way in Holloway Prison.

The A24 fifty-pound notes were rapidly becoming too hot to handle. On the day that searches were being carried out at all the addresses of the gang's associates, an elderly woman in West Kingsdown found a Tesco shopping bag of £50,000 in fifty-pound notes among the tomato plants in her garden. It is no surprise that the notes all started with the A24 prefix and, although it was close to Noye's sister's garden, it must have been coincidence, for when she faced trial for receiving the cash, the jury found her not guilty.

On the evening of 30 January 1985, at Aachen on the border between Belgium and Germany, German border guards were enjoying a quiet coffee when up came a Mercedes 500 car with English registration plates and a middle-aged English couple inside. A quick check of their passports identified them as John and Anne Elcombe from Peckham in south London. All good law enforcement officers acquire a gut feeling, a taste, a smell and a sense that something isn't right, and this was one of those nights. The officer concerned just knew the car and the man didn't belong together, and it was decided to search the vehicle. The rear seat was taken out and there, in the cavity underneath, were lots of beautifully-wrapped bricks. The officers' immediate thought was drugs, but when they removed the wrapping, they found cash, not cocaine, in unused British fifty-pound notes. Bundle after bundle was pulled out of the car and, on closer examination, all the numbers started with A24. In excess of £700,000 was removed from the car.

Details were passed to Interpol, which in turn contacted Scotland Yard. When results came back, the German officers, who had assumed the money was counterfeit, were amazed to find the notes were genuine and had recently been issued by the Bank of England to Barclays Bank cash centre in Bristol. The Elcombes were not wanted and the car was registered to one Gordon Parry. It transpired that Anne Elcombe was a cousin of Parry's common-law wife.

The Elcombes said this was their life savings, which they were taking to Switzerland to take advantage of an investment opportunity. No crime, no foul so the money was returned to them and they continued their journey. Later the Elcombes were arrested and tried at the Old Bailey where their story changed. Their defence was that they were innocent couriers being paid with a free holiday to transport the money to a bank in Zurich. It came as no surprise when, after hearing how this respectful, middle-aged couple had been so cruelly duped by their villainous relatives, the jury found them not guilty.

The trial of Noye for the murder of John Fordham commenced in November 1985, ten months after that fateful night. It seemed inevitable that the jury would find him guilty as no one had ever been acquitted having been charged with killing a police officer.

Noye had offered Detective Chief Superintendent Boyce £1 million, which he would place in a bank account anywhere in the world, if he could be allowed to plead guilty to manslaughter. I sat and listened to Noye offering to reveal every detail of the gold-laundering operation, and promising to help recover the remaining gold during an informal meeting between Noye and a senior officer – a fellow mason – in the cells at Lambeth Court. We had a final chance to recover the gold in return for Noye pleading guilty to manslaughter. That was never going to happen. How could there ever be any other verdict but guilty?

Money buys the very best and Noye used his wealth to instruct the best defence team he could possibly assemble, led by the eminent John Mathew QC. A wonderful defence strategy was concocted, which would paint Noye as the victim. He would plead not guilty and claim self-defence. He was, after all, just a man defending his family and his castle against an unprovoked attack by police who had illegally entered his property. The fact that Noye admitted killing John ruled out the charge of manslaughter and meant that he could only be tried for murder. However, Mathew produced an eloquent story of fact and fantasy, and Noye was pronounced not guilty. Noye thanked the jury and told them he was indeed an innocent man.

Months later Noye again stood trial at the Old Bailey, charged with handling the gold bullion. This time the jury found him guilty and Noye told the jury he hoped they all died of cancer. He was given thirteen years. In 1996, two years after his release, he became England's first road-rage killer when he stabbed Stephen Cameron to death on the M25. He was sentenced to life imprisonment.

Chapter 13

In The Heat of the Action

Back at the Brink's office, all manner of information was coming in from informants, who suddenly knew things they had not previously mentioned. Telephone intercepts were buzzing as the criminals chatted to one another and there were lots of calls from the public who, having read the newspapers, were, with the best intentions, remembering incidents that they thought might be related. The workload was increasing daily.

Among the large amount of information coming from the telephone wires was a conversation between two criminals laughing about their 'goldmine' in Sierra Leone in Africa. They even mentioned the name of their company. Enquiries revealed a very prosperous company whose importation of gold was running at many thousands of pounds per month, a company that had only been incorporated a few weeks after the Brink's robbery. We needed to pursue this, but the chances of carrying out an inquiry ourselves or getting a response to a request for help from this troubled African nation was somewhere south of nil.

A cup of coffee provided the solution. We dropped in at Brixton Police Station for a chat with my previous governor and, in passing, mentioned the problems of getting information from Sierra Leone. With a smile on his face he said, 'You know it's not what, it's who' and picked up the phone. A few minutes later he said, 'You haven't got time to sit here drinking coffee, you have an appointment with the *chargé d'affaires* at the Sierra Leone Embassy in Portland Place in one hour.' Within an hour, we were sitting at a huge, beautifully-inlaid, oak desk, behind which was a leather-back chair containing an elegant gentleman whose appearance was not what we had anticipated. Lebanese of origin, his hands moved from finger to finger as he fiddled with the world's largest worry beads. Each bead was a solid gold nugget.

A servant laid out a tray of aromatic teas and we were asked to explain our predicament. The *chargé d'affaires* then picked up the phone and within minutes was speaking to Sierra Leone's Chief of Police, Bambay Kamara. We were told: 'Everything is arranged, you will be protected at all times by Mr Mohamed's men and everything you need will be provided. The presidential jet is flying back to Freetown in two days' time and you are welcome to accompany the president.'

Imagining a flight of luxury, we returned to Scotland Yard where we were brought back to earth with the senior officers concluding, rightly, that we could not be seen to be beholden to anyone. They did, however, decide that two of us should go and see what we could find, so we packed for Sierra Leone.

As we entered the arrival hall at Freetown Airport, we noticed a tiny man holding a card with my name on. He introduced himself as Sergeant Barr, the Sierra Leone Interpol officer. Expecting him to transport us to a hotel, we were surprised when he pointed to another group of people who were also holding a card with my name on. 'Those are Mr Mohamed's men, they will be looking after you,' he said. It appeared that Mr Mohamed was far more important than the police force. We were escorted to a new Range Rover and, as soon as we sat down, a cooler box was opened, and we were offered beer, spirits and cold sodas of every description. As we drove away, we saw Sergeant Barr getting into a rusty old Cortina with bald tyres.

We drove through scenes of abject poverty before arriving at a luxury hotel and told that we would be collected after breakfast the following morning. Chief of Police Kamara (who, sadly, would be murdered in the 1991 civil war) came to see us and suggested that we would be better served by allowing Mr Mohamed's men to see to our every need. It appeared that that whoever Mr Mohamed was, he was capable of giving us better protection than the actual police and we intended to stick close to his men.

Next morning I flicked through the local paper and saw the headline: 'Cannibals Eat School Teacher at Mile 95'. We were collected as promised and taken to a downtown office where we were introduced to an unnamed Lebanese gentleman of obvious importance. Our problem was discussed and we were assured that it would be resolved in no time. We sat at the rear of a large room, and were attended to by a waiter who brought us plates upon plates of food until our unnamed gentleman came back to us and said, 'I am just arranging for your safe passage in the territory you wish to visit. That area is the territory governed by the Whip in the House. I have sent for him, but as the House is sitting, it may take a little longer.' A couple of hours later, the member of parliament came in and was most apologetic to our man with no name. Then an arsenal of weapons, including handguns, rifles and automatic weapons, were laid out on the table. 'What would you prefer?' we were asked. I explained as tactfully as possible that with a car of fully-armed men in front, two more in the car with us and another car with four more armed men behind, we had never felt so safe in our whole lives. This seemed to appease everyone and we were escorted back to our hotel to await tomorrow's adventure.

The following day dawned hot and humid, and we were relieved to be sitting in the Range Rover, which was air-conditioned. It was nine hours each way so an overnight stay had been arranged in the home of a diamond-mine manager. After hours dodging the pot holes in the roads and seeing nothing but trees and the occasional corrugated roofed shack, the landscape became more barren until there were nothing but a vast expanse of sandy soil with holes in the ground. Some were filled with water while others were dried out by the baking sun, and in every hole with water there were four or five people up to their knees, shovelling and sifting the soil as it was placed into their shaking sieves. These were the diamond fields of Sierra Leone and there were thousands of people hoping to find that one diamond that might change their lives.

We travelled for hours until eventually arriving at a river bank. A few shacks, some purporting to be shops, could be seen about 200 yards away. This was Tembecki Junction we were told. Looking around we could not

see why or to what it was junctioned. We looked down to a wide river bed
with just the gentlest flow of muddy water meandering down the middle.
There, bizarrely dressed in a suit and tie, was the member of parliament
we had met the previous day. Waving his hands towards the river bank he
said: 'There is your goldmine, but only this side of the river.' In his hands
were copies of all the paperwork relating to the registered company we
were hunting. The company had the right to prospect an area of land
30 square metres from the centre of the river. The banks had been dug
heavily and the land was potmarked with holes from years of hopeless
endeavour. Any hope of finding gold had evaporated long before the
registration of our London-based company. Yet we knew there would be
invoices to say that the gold had come from here, when in fact it had come
from the robbery. We'd gone all that way to find just another method of
disguising the funds generated by the Brink's-Mat gold.

The telephone intercepts were yielding fruit in many different ways
and one day a voice was recorded from a phone in Spain. The recipient
of the call had been targeted because he was the best friend of John
Fleming, one of the suspected original robbers. Fleming, a well-known
and very active armed robber, had been photographed by surveillance
officers meeting with McAvoy, Robinson and other members of the gang.
These meetings had taken place months before the actual robbery so it
was obvious something was being planned, but at the time there was no
way of knowing what. Since the robbery Fleming had not been seen at
any of his usual haunts. His wife was still at their home, but all enquiries
into his whereabouts had been unsuccessful. Officers who knew Fleming
listened to the recordings of the call from Spain and were certain they
had found his hiding place.

There were no official working practices with the Spanish Police and
English officers had no authority to conduct their own enquiries on
Spanish soil. But times were different in those days and there was always a
way. Detective Superintendent Lundy had a friend in a senior position in
the Spanish police and a couple of days after identifying Fleming's voice,
Lundy assembled four of us and said, 'We're off to Spain.' Somehow he

had got official blessing for us to identify Fleming and his house, and to allow us to monitor his phones and place listening devices in his home.

It didn't take long to find him. He owned a four-bedroomed house, built into the cliffside in a beautiful area of Mascarat, Altea. This was one of the more expensive developments on the coast, with views down to the marina and the sea, and just ten minutes drive from the bright lights and bars of Alicante. On the very first night Fleming went off drinking. We knew from the telephone calls we were intercepting between Fleming and his friends back in England that he would be drinking for hours, and would almost certainly return in the early hours with a lady on his arm ready to earn her fee for a night's entertainment. With him out of the way, we bugged the lounge, bedroom and balcony, which overlooked the sea, and was his favourite place to sit and talk on the phone.

Little did we realize that it would take one phone call to unlock a new world of money laundering, drug cartels and drug smuggling of epic proportions; one phone call that would transport me to a new adventure on a tiny island in the Caribbean Sea. But I'm jumping the gun so let's get back to Fleming.

Among his many calls to friends, most of which relayed his sexual conquests, there was one to an organization called Comprehensive Company Management Ltd in the Isle of Man. It became apparent that this company was running a large investment portfolio on Fleming's behalf and involved far too much money for an unemployed criminal to have acquired legitimately. There was also mention of a visit from an acquaintance of Fleming's referred to as Enrico. Back in London, enquiries revealed the company was owned by a solicitor named Patrick Diamond. An intercept was placed on Diamond's phone.

A couple of days later, a call was received by Diamond from our unknown Enrico, requesting that Diamond travel to London with £50,000 cash to give to him. They arranged a meeting at the Hilton Hotel in London, which took place under the watchful eyes of a surveillance team from Scotland Yard. It was important to find the identity of Enrico and he was followed to a bank where he was observed going to the vaults.

Leaving there he travelled to Heathrow Airport and checked in for a flight to Paris. There, he was stopped and searched, and was found to be holding an American passport in the name of Steven Marzovilla as well as a large knife, and so he was arrested for possession of an offensive weapon. Among his other possessions was a key for a safety deposit box.

Officers quickly obtained a search warrant for the box and, when they opened it, they found part of the £50,000 given to him by Diamond and another passport in the name of Scott Errico. A check on that name revealed police were now holding one of America's most wanted.

Errico was described by US authorities as the enforcer of a south Florida drug-smuggling ring, which was responsible for the importation of $700-million worth of marijuana using luxury yachts cruising in and out of Amity Yacht Center in Fort Lauderdale. The ring was headed by a man named Raymond 'Little Ray' Thompson and one day in 1980, an argument took place between the gang as two of the members, Robert Vogt and William Harris, had decided that they were going to leave. The two men were taken miles out to sea off the Florida coast where Errico shot them both in the head, tied them to heavy anchors and tossed them into the sea. The bodies were never recovered. Thompson pleaded guilty to the murders, but the jury failed to agree on Errico and he was bailed to appear at a later retrial. Immediately he went on the run and it was two years before he reappeared on the streets of London.

He was also wanted for the murder of James Savoy, a friend of Thompson's who stole $500,000 from him, only for a prostitute to steal it from Savoy. Again Errico got rid of him in the middle of the sea. Back in London, Errico was quick to seek a deal for himself. He would admit the murders and the drugs charges, and would agree to be extradited back to America 'provided', as he put it, 'I won't fry' (in the electric chair). He was sentenced to two life imprisonments and given a release date in fifty years' time when he will be 82-years-old.

Back in Spain the authorities attempting to assist the British police arrested Fleming and deported him. At that time there was no extradition treaty between England and Spain, and it was for the deportee to decide his next destination. Fleming boarded a flight to the USA, but was detained at immigration and again deported. This time he flew to Costa Rica where he would spend the next few years.

The Brink's–Mat inquiry was so big and the participants had so many criminal activities elsewhere in the world that it was starting to drift away from the original robbery, although this was still being heavily investigated in London. The Brink's squad had split into two, with one half headed by Detective Chief Superintendent Boyce and the other by Detective Superintendent Lundy. Both had their own ways of doing things.

Lundy decided it was time to take a good look at Patrick Diamond, so a search warrant was obtained and a group of officers travelled to the Isle of Man. Diamond was arrested and taken to the local police station. Like Relton, Diamond had no desire to spend any time in a police cell, and soon decided he would much rather sit in the interrogation room and tell his life history. It wasn't long before he confessed his part in knowingly laundering the proceeds of the Brink's robbery for the benefit of Fleming. He had hidden hundreds of thousands of pounds for him in obscure companies and had done the same for Errico. During Diamond's interview came a chance remark that would yet again turn everyone's life upside down.

'I'm just a beginner at this laundering lark,' said Diamond. When the interviewing officers asked what he meant by that, he said, 'Well, the best money launderer I have ever met is located out in the BVI.' Not wanting to appear ignorant, but having no idea what BVI meant, we encouraged him to continue in the hope that all would be revealed. Diamond was on a roll and he told the officer of a man named Sean Murphy who had a company named Financial Management and Trust in Tortola, the largest of the BVI, by which he meant the British Virgin Islands. 'He even has the chief minister as a partner to add credibility to his operation,' said Diamond breezily. He told us that he had met Murphy through a Miami-based lawyer named Michael Levine who had contacted him to set up companies to hide tax money. Diamond would fly to America, meet with Levine in his office and often leave with a suitcase containing $100,000.

Then he would jump on a plane back to England and deposit the money into the accounts he had set up. Often when he went to America, Murphy would be in Levine's office filling up a suitcase with similar amounts of cash. The maximum amount of cash that could be taken out of the USA was just $10,000, but not once had either Murphy or Diamond been stopped on departure.

Not many of us had any knowledge of the British Virgin Islands, but a bit of reading up revealed that, together with Turks and Caicos, Anguilla and Montserrat, they were the only British dependencies left in the Caribbean. There was a British governor and the islands were run democratically with an elected parliament headed by a chief minister. The police force was headed by a British former police chief and the laws were basically the same as in the UK.

There was no way Lundy was going to miss this one, and meetings were arranged with representatives from the Foreign and Commonwealth Office as well as the Yard's legal department. It was eventually decided that a team of officers – which included Lundy and me – should present themselves to the commissioner of police there, without prior warning, and ask for assistance. The population of the main island, Tortola, was not much over 10,000 and it was believed to be a very close community. We couldn't take the chance of our arrival being talked about before we got there.

There was no direct flight to Tortola so it was London to Miami and then down to St Thomas in the US Virgin Islands, and on to the '*Bomba Charger*', a wonderfully-named ferry, which spluttered its way, belching smoke, to the west end of Tortola. I was in a state of wonderment. A balmy breeze kept the temperatures comfortable and the seas were a beautiful turquoise blue with myriad colourful fish wherever you looked. Pristine beaches ran down to the sea from each island we passed with not a soul on them. This surely must be heaven.

We booked into the *Treasure Island Hotel*, which was situated on the hillside close to the centre of Road Town, the capital of the BVI. Never one to waste time, Lundy went straight to Road Town Police Station where he was quickly shown into the office of Commissioner of Police R.J. Bretherton. Lundy laid out his mission, which was not something that Bretherton, who had been commissioner since 1981 and was fast approaching the end of his tenure, was wanting or expecting. By the time he left the office some forty minutes later, not only had Lundy been made a special constable, but he was also in possession of a search warrant for Murphy's office and home. The rest of us were summoned to police headquarters where we were also sworn in as special constables of The Royal Virgin Islands Police Force. By the time all these formalities had been completed it was 7.00 pm and even Lundy, who was champing at the bit to get started, was forced to relax, and enjoy a meal and a rum punch in preparation for what promised to be a long day tomorrow.

Early birds don't always catch the worm, but this time a 5.00 am knock on a front door bore fruit, as a sleepy-eyed Murphy opened the door to five rather large detectives from Scotland Yard. Lundy did the introductions and the moment he said 'from Scotland Yard', the colour drained from Murphy's face, and he collapsed into a large recliner and buried his face in his hands. When Lundy waved the search warrant in Murphy's face he became a blubbering wreck. This was obviously not going to be the hardest interrogation any of us had ever undertaken. Lundy explained the reason for us being there and when he said Diamond had been arrested, Murphy realized that he was in big trouble. He wanted to tell us everything, but Lundy had to stop him. Lundy wanted it all, but needed Murphy to start at the beginning.

Murphy was a qualified accountant of Irish extract who had worked for a number of corporate accountancy companies. On one particular assignment he had been sent to the British Virgin Islands and been introduced to Chief Minister Cyril B. Romney. During the course of this meeting, Romney had mentioned the opportunities that presented themselves for someone wanting to open up a business forming and registering companies in the BVI. Murphy recognized the opportunity that had just presented itself and a few months later, in 1980, he opened

the offices of Financial Management and Trust in the centre of Road
Town. His silent partner in the venture was Cyril B. Romney.

Business was steady but nothing wonderful until, out of the blue,
Murphy received a telephone call from a lawyer in Miami. A meeting was
held between the pair and Murphy returned to Tortola with a suitcase
containing $100,000, which he deposited at Road Town's branch of
Barclays Bank in the account of a newly-formed company. His reputation
spread and it wasn't long before he was being contacted by lawyers
representing drug organizations across the USA. He was being flown to
the States regularly where drug dealers, awash with money, entertained
him with lavish parties. Murphy enjoyed the lifestyle, with the endless
booze, women and cocaine, and before long he was in too deep and unable
to say no to any requests to assist these men. Soon his trips to the States
to pick up cash, one suitcase at a time, became too time consuming and
he decided on a plan that wouldn't look out of place in any crime thriller.

At a prearranged time he would jump into a dinghy that he owned and
set off to a deserted island, lay out a coloured towel to identify himself and
await the arrival of a small aircraft. The plane would not land, but would
make a flying pass of the island and, as it reached Murphy, a suitcase,
bound and wrapped in plastic to ensure that it was waterproof, would
be thrown out of the plane for him to recover. Murphy would collect
the suitcase, take it home and remove hundreds of thousands of dollars,
which were stuffed inside. He would then go down to Barclays Bank and
deposit the cash.

This story was so incredible that the officers found it hard to believe.
Realizing their scepticism, Murphy got up and, gesturing at them to
follow him, led them to the basement of the house where there were
dozens of suitcases of every size and colour. Some were damaged, but all
had the belts that had been used to secure them.

Nothing Murphy said from now on would surprise them, but within
minutes eyebrows were raised when he told them that, as Barclays Bank
was taking so long to count his money, he had purchased a counting
machine and presented it to the manager. Then he said the bank was

charging a 2 per cent fee to deposit money. Surely no one would pay to deposit money and no one would charge unless both parties were aware that the money was not legitimate.

Despite all his riches, Murphy was becoming overwhelmed and had begun to realize that he was in a precarious situation. He was involved with heavy criminals and the threat of violence was never far away. The money was still flooding in and, like King Canute, he just couldn't turn the tide. Perhaps the arrival of the police would be his lifeline.

We didn't know how we were going to deal with offences of this magnitude in Tortola. There was neither the manpower nor the expertise to carry out the enquiries, and most of the offences related to drug smuggling in the USA. First it was necessary to get Murphy charged with something and brought before the court, as this would allow him to be remanded into our custody. He was remanded with stringent conditions, which placed him under curfew, only allowing him to leave his home when accompanied by a police officer. With Murphy's help, we were now able to continue searching through the hundreds of registered companies in his office. We also moved into Murphy's home. His wife had no idea what he had been up to and, as well as coming to terms with his pending incarceration, she also had to deal with a house full of people who were destroying the luxurious life she had started to take for granted.

On the first night at the house, two of the officers were preparing to go to bed when Murphy came into the room holding a baseball bat. 'It's OK,' he said, aware that the officers may think he'd changed his tune and was about to get violent. 'This is for you to deal with the tarantulas.' It wasn't the most peaceful night's sleep they had ever had.

Before any decision could be made about what to do with Murphy, there was also the small matter of interviewing Chief Minister Romney. We wanted to keep this as low profile as possible and certainly didn't want to arrest him publicly. With the help of the governor of the islands, we requested that Romney attend the governor's house for a meeting.

The governor's residence enjoys an elevated location overlooking the clear blue waters of the Caribbean Sea. Lundy and I were watching the white sails filling with breeze from the trade winds when the governor brought Romney in to the room and left us to chat. It soon became apparent that Romney was a silent partner in every way. The only part he played was to inspect his bank balance to see how much money Murphy had deposited for him that month. Even though the deposits were getting larger each time, he had no idea about Murphy's involvements and there was no way he could be held accountable for anything other than naivety.

Predictably in such a small community, rumours were starting to spread. Romney was accused of owning 99 per cent of Murphy's company (which wasn't true, although his holding was significantly more than half) and his opponents called for a vote of no confidence in him. However, before this could take place, Romney asked the governor to dissolve parliament, which he duly did. Elections were held shortly afterwards and, to nobody's surprise, the charismatic Romney was returned to a seat in parliament, although not that of chief minister.

Lundy was doing his best to melt the phone lines, with calls to the Drug Enforcement Administration (DEA) in Miami, where he tried to get someone to appreciate the value that Murphy could be to their investigation into major drug organizations. The response was lukewarm but eventually it was agreed that, should Lundy get Murphy to Miami, they would provide assistance in his debriefing, and an office and agents would be made available in Fort Lauderdale. The idea was put to Murphy, and he agreed to go to America and co-operate with the authorities there. Murphy was taken back before the local court where the charges were dropped as he had agreed to this course of action. Time to pick up our beds and relocate to the good old US of A.

Our new office was a room, 15ft square, with a couple of desks, a couple of phones, half a dozen chairs, and two tired and bored DEA agents, together with a typewriter and a middle-aged woman sitting behind it painting her nails. We knew Lundy well and one look at his face was enough to know that this was not the time for conversation. He picked up the phone to speak to whoever he had been dealing with, and, as we were later informed, he was told in no uncertain manner that that was all the help they had available and that was all we were getting. Lundy was not the most diplomatic of people and, slamming down the phone, he looked at us and said, 'Hold the fort. I'll be back sometime tomorrow' and walked out of the room.

Lundy never told us exactly what happened, but I know he was upset and angry that the DEA didn't seem to be taking him seriously. Perhaps he spent all day on the phone, but the better theory is that he jumped on a plane and flew to the DEA headquarters in Springfield, Virginia, where he could rattle a few doors. When we asked, Lundy just smiled and said, 'Let's see what tomorrow brings.'

Tomorrow certainly delivered. When we arrived at the DEA building we were shown to a suite of offices where a senior agent was awaiting our arrival. There were about ten DEA agents, and a couple of agents from alcohol and tobacco as well as treasury agents, FBI and firearms. There were profilers, typists, phones, desks and computers with operators because we didn't know how to use them, and a couple of rooms for extra offices. It wasn't a case of finding a desk and a chair, but rather take your pick and have two if you want.

Introductions were made and Lundy gave his first briefing. Everything now depended on Murphy and his memory as he picked his way through the boxes of files we had brought from his office. He didn't disappoint. Some companies needed two or more signatures before anything could be done so they were put to one side, but many were under Murphy's sole control. There were millions of dollars in countless accounts. He explained that as deposits of $10,000 or more required proof that the funds were legitimate, many drug dealers paid people to walk into banks and deposit cash a few dollars short of $10,000. These couriers would visit every bank in their town and surrounding area, and make as many deposits in a day as banking hours would allow. Interestingly, the British law that requires you to prove money is legitimate if you want to deposit more than £10,000 was introduced in the wake of the Brink's-Mat inquiry when it was shown how easy it was to move around large sums of cash, which were the proceeds of crime.

Vast amounts of money held in these accounts were signed over to the US Government and in the first couple of days, with a stroke of Murphy's pen and his flowery signature, the US Treasury became richer by $50 million or more. Suddenly our American cousins started to take us seriously.

We were naive in those days and none of us were computer literate. We knew nothing of hard drives or floppy disks and, as far as I knew, pixels were still living at the bottom of the garden. All our files relating to Murphy and money laundering were typed or handwritten, and we didn't understand how money could be pinged around the world at the touch of a button. Murphy was a wonderful, patient teacher and we were eager pupils. He taught us enough to gain a university degree in the art of money laundering and drug smuggling.

At that time, the law in America was much stronger than in Britain, especially where drugs were concerned. If you could go to court and prove to a judge that there was a strong possibility something had been obtained from the proceeds of drugs, a search and seizure warrant was issued. It was then the responsibility of the owner of that property to prove these assets were not drug related. Rarely did the drug dealers make a counter claim. They had so much money stashed away elsewhere that they treated these seizures as collateral damage. What did it matter if the authorities took their Lamborghini? It was about time they tried out a Ferrari anyway.

We learned a new way of policing. Seize it first and worry about it later. From the Errico/Thompson papers alone there were houses, ranches and apartment buildings seized in double-quick time. There was even a shopping centre! Murphy's evidence led the investigators to at least ten major drug cartels in the US and also uncovered links to drug cartels in Colombia. Almost without exception, each cartel investigated included at its very core a high-profile lawyer. It would take four years to complete all the court cases that resulted from Murphy's information and evidence. During that time, numerous major drug dealers (and even one of Florida's most feared defence attorneys) were imprisoned.

The stories that were uncovered are worthy of a book on their own, but a few of the tales deserve a brief summary and are great examples of the vast wealth that was being generated by the drug cartels across America.

Fred Carroll and Thomas McNichols were well-educated university graduates who started dealing cannabis in a small way, but they had big ideas and by the early 1980s were bringing in marijuana by the ton. They were buying direct from Colombia and were brazen enough to have cargo ships dock in the middle of Boston Harbour to be unloaded. Even more brazenly, they would transfer the drugs to Boston's grand Horticultural Hall, where an employee would let them in after hours, and the drugs would be weighed and distributed with all transactions entered in a ledger. By morning the building would open for business as if nothing had happened.

On a trip to the Caribbean they met Murphy and he became their man to launder the money. They invested wisely, and were soon buying property in the exclusive and expensive Back Bay area of Boston. By the time our investigation had caught up with them, they had left the drug trade behind and were rich from legitimate property deals. McNichols' girlfriend only agreed to marry him after he promised her that he was out of the drug business for good; it was Murphy who flew to Boston to take the wedding photos.

Unfortunately, with Murphy's help, their past caught up with them and in 1988 they pleaded guilty to drug smuggling and money laundering, were given lengthy prison sentences and had most of their assets confiscated.

Randy Lanier was a promising racing driver who had driven at both The 24 Hours of Daytona and The 24 Hours of Le Mans. After leaving the team for which he was driving, he reappeared in 1984 with his own team called Blue Thunder Racing. It isn't cheap to run a racing team and a season's cost can amount to $750,000. The racing fraternity wondered who on earth was sponsoring this race-winning team. Around the same time, Ben Kramer, the World Offshore Powerboat Champion, was competing in powerboat racing with his team Apache. This was another expensive sport, yet Apache had no apparent sponsor.

Murphy was to provide the answer as he had laundered millions of dollars for Kramer and Lanier who were working together. Kramer purchased hundreds of tons of cannabis from Colombia, which was imported through an unidentified third party by tugboats and barges landing at New York, San Francisco and New Orleans. Once safely ashore, Lanier took over the distribution and with his vast network covering Louisiana, Virginia, California, Florida and Kentucky, he was able to sell his wares as fast as it could be landed. Assets seized from Lanier amounted to almost $150 million.

Lanier was arrested, but before he could be tried he went on the run, and it was two years before he was captured in Antigua and brought back to face trial. Both men were convicted and sentenced to life imprisonment, and Kramer was also convicted of manslaughter in an unrelated matter. In 1989, Kramer was serving his sentence in a high-security prison just outside Miami when one day, during morning exercise, a two-seater Bell helicopter flew in under the radar and hovered over the exercise yard. Kramer ran, jumped and hung onto the helicopter's runners, but the pilot couldn't gain enough height and crashed into the perimeter fence, breaking both his legs and Kramer's ankle. Kramer is still in prison while Lanier was released on licence in 2014.

Some of Murphy's clients had wanted their wealth to be spread between the various firms specializing in company formation. Murphy had built up good relationships with several of these and had sent them a few of his clients. These companies trusted Murphy and had no idea that they were facilitating the movement of the proceeds of drugs. One internationally-renowned company was horrified when we visited them, armed with a search warrant, and were ready, willing and able to assist in any way possible.

We were travelling back and forth to the BVI to deal with the investigation and one morning, in Tortola, two of us came across an account called White Sail, which had funds in excess of $4 million. The owner was a former US marine and Murphy just happened to have his passport in the safe of his office in Road Town. That lunchtime, as we climbed the stairs on our return to the office, a rather large gentleman with blond crew-cut hair stood aside to let us pass. Returning to the paperwork for White Sail, I asked one of the partners when he had last dealt with this client. 'About five minutes ago,' he said. 'He's just walked out. He was asking if I knew where Murphy was.' Realizing we had passed our man on the stairs, we rushed out and headed for Murphy's office. There, looking in the window and banging on the door was our marine. Apologizing for not being there for him, we unlocked the front door and explained that Murphy was on holiday and that we were looking after matters for him.

He said that he had come down to the islands to collect his passport. We asked how he got here without a passport, and he said he'd hired a small boat and its owner to bring him over from St Thomas in the US Virgin Islands. He told us his name and we opened the safe and removed his passport. 'Is this yours, Sir?' we asked. 'Yes,' he said, 'that's me.' 'In that case,' we replied, 'you are under arrest for drugs offences and money laundering.' He was cautioned and struck dumb as the colour drained from his weather-beaten face. We escorted him to Road Town Police Station, locked him in a cell and then worked out what to do. The laws of the BVI were almost the same as in Britain, but had not been updated for years. There was certainly nothing to cover money laundering unless we reverted to 'fraudulently obtaining' or something along those lines. We could always ask him if he would return voluntarily to the US to face charges, but he was hardly going to agree to that. And if he refused, we faced months of paperwork and court appearances in an attempt to extradite him to America. We could certainly get him thrown off the islands as he had entered illegally, but what good was that to us? The old saying, 'there is more than one way to skin a cat', came to mind and a couple of hours later, we'd come up with a plan.

We brought him up to be interviewed. We explained that we'd checked his details and found that he was wanted in America on various cases of drug smuggling. The truth was we could find no criminal record for him anywhere. We also said that we'd gone through Murphy's records and found that he was the registered owner of a company that had $4.8 million banked assets. That bit was true. 'I have no idea what you are talking about, Sir,' he replied. We told him in that case, we'd have to prove it through the courts and we'd apply for extradition, during which time he would be remanded in custody in Road Town Prison. If our application was successful, he would be returned to face trial in America. 'Of course, you could always volunteer to go back,' I said. He declined our offer. We said that was fine and we would prepare the charges, but as we were in the Caribbean, where things move at a slower pace, it would be at least a year before the case was heard. And then, laughingly, I added: 'Of course, you say there is nothing here for you other than your passport so you could always get in your little boat and sail away. The only trouble is, if you are lying to us and that $4.8 million is yours, you will never see it again.'

Half an hour after we'd returned him to his cell, the desk sergeant rang to tell us the prisoner wanted to see us. 'Sir,' he said, 'you have been very fair with me. I was wondering if you could take me down to the quay where my boat is waiting and allow me to leave the island. There is nothing here for me.'

It was late afternoon when we got to the dockside and met his boatman. The marine told the boatman to fill up with petrol as it was time for them to leave. 'We can't leave now,' said the boatman, 'it's getting dark and I have no running lights.' 'Oh we are leaving, believe me,' said the marine, whose tone of voice and icy look had the boatman scurrying away with a petrol can in his hands to find his fuel. 'May I buy you a beer?' asked the marine. We nodded and he returned with cans of Budweiser. We sat at the dockside and he told us that he'd learned a very expensive lesson that day. He said he'd had a good run and it was time for him to settle down. We asked him about the yacht that was also registered to his company. 'Don't waste your time looking for that as she's at the bottom of the sea,' he said. 'She was getting too well known.' Jumping into the boat, he turned and with a smile said, 'Thank you again, gentlemen. Thank God I listened to my mother. She always told me never to put all my eggs in one basket.'

All that was left to do was to get Murphy and his magic pen to sign over the $4.8 million to the BVI Treasury. That was about 20 per cent of the annual budget for the islands at that time. What started back in London as a search for the gold had led to international money laundering of epic proportions. Years later the British Government would receive a multi million dollar payment from the proceeds of the investigation.

As for the rest of the gold that was stolen in the Brink's-Mat robbery, some of it is out there somewhere. But the vast majority is sitting comfortably around the fingers or necks of anyone who has purchased gold since 1985.

Chapter 14

Policing Paradise

Back in London I got the call I didn't want. I had been promoted to chief inspector and was on my way to a desk on the second floor of Catford Police Station in south London. I had been spoiled for too long doing proactive police work and my days of fun were surely over. I had five years left before retirement and I seemed destined to spend that time bored out of my brains, overseeing the day-to-day running of the CID offices of Catford, Lee Road and Sydenham.

A chief inspector's position must be the most tedious job in the police force. It is a supervisory position, which involves checking other people's investigations and telling them how to proceed on each inquiry. But sitting behind a desk and dealing with paperwork is not my idea of fun. I missed the action. Hours of meetings to discuss policing policy, strategy, money, action plans, racial equality, positive discrimination, how much money was available for officers' overtime and, most importantly, political correctness, just didn't stimulate my brain or get my juices flowing. We were starting on a slippery slope. The most important thing was no longer fighting crime and the protection of the public; now it was how to police without offending anyone.

I sought my thrills elsewhere, namely on the tennis court. While still at Clapham I had taken two weeks' leave and attended a course at Bisham Abbey in an attempt to gain the highest tennis coaching qualification. Again, my legendary luck prevailed and I walked away as a Lawn Tennis Association-certified professional tennis coach. It was always my intention that, on retirement, I would keep busy but do nothing related to police work. Coaching tennis looked like a good idea and, in preparation, we sold our house and bought a smaller bungalow with a big garden in Sevenoaks,

Kent. With the money left over we had a hard tennis court built and I started coaching on my occasional days off. Now my real enjoyment was not being at work but in the back garden, coaching promising youngsters that I had taken under my wing. Then I saw an advert for a job in the British Virgin Islands.

R. J. Bretherton had retired as the BVI's commissioner of police and his successor, Ronald Thompson, former assistant chief constable in Northumberland, had only been in the hot seat for a few months when he concluded that he needed someone to come out to the islands and form a drug squad. His force didn't have the expertise to investigate enquiries relating to money laundering and, most importantly, no one was dealing with the drug smugglers and the drugs, which were coming to the islands.

The normal route at that time was to ask the Foreign Office to fund a British officer to come out as an advisor. But it was well known that if an officer goes to an overseas post to advise, he usually ends up sitting in a poky office with no one to talk to but himself. You can only advise on what you are told and if you are told nothing your position is untenable. But Thompson's request was different. He requested that a British officer be funded to work, not as an advisor, but as a member of the force. The job was to train a newly-formed drug squad and lead the squad operationally: to get his hands dirty and lead by example. A new rank of assistant superintendent would be created so that no position would be lost to the current officers. This request was granted and the new post was advertised across all UK police forces. I saw it, and that night I turned to my wife and said, jokingly, 'Fancy a year or two in the Caribbean?' to which she replied, 'Yes please.' The next morning I sat down and completed my application.

A few weeks later I was informed I had been put on a shortlist of five and would be called before a selection board in the near future. When I arrived for the interview, I was thrilled to learn that Thompson was on the board. It was fortunate that he knew me and I was certainly the only candidate that had actually been to the British Virgin Islands. Everything seemed to be in my favour and the only person who could possibly mess this up was me, but luckily I didn't and the next day I accepted the offer of a two-year contract. Goodbye desk, it was back to a little bit of excitement.

The islands are actually called the Virgin Islands; the 'British' is only added to stop confusion with the United States Virgin Islands, which are in very close proximity. It is said that with a strong arm and a following wind, it is possible to throw a cricket ball across The Narrows, the channel of water that separates the two, from Little Thatch to St John, therefore throwing from Britain to America. The main island of Tortola is twelve miles long and three miles across, and, in 1987, when I went out, there was a population of approximately 10,000, with another 3,000 people living on the other islands, mainly Virgin Gorda, Anegada and Jost Van Dyke. A few other islands were inhabited, including Necker, which had been bought by Richard Branson to create his Caribbean island paradise.

The islands were prospering due to three main industries. The first was sailing: marinas sprang up to cater for the increasing demand for sailboat chartering, and the gentle trade winds made the seas a mecca for the ever-growing yacht community. Secondly, the cruise ship industry was booming and Tortola was one of those destinations rich in sun, sea and golden sands, which the vast liners loved to visit. The third was offshore company formation and banking, as wealthy people put their assets into companies that benefited from more favourable tax breaks than they would receive in their own jurisdiction.

We arrived on Tortola in the first week of July 1987, and settled into my old haunt, the *Treasure Island Hotel*. The first few days were taken up with finding somewhere to live and being introduced to the close-knit expat community. That first Saturday we were invited to someone's house to watch Pat Cash beat Ivan Lendl in the Wimbledon final, although it was not quite the same in black and white, especially with an intermittent signal. When Monday morning arrived, it was time to find my way to the police station, meet my newly-selected drug squad and get my feet under the table.

The Royal Virgin Island Police Force was relatively young, having been inaugurated just twenty years earlier in 1967. Prior to that, the islands had been policed by the British Leeward Island Police who were responsible for all the British territories in the Caribbean. The force consisted of just over 100 officers, half of whom were born locally and half of whom came from other islands. My team was to consist of Tortola-born Detective Station Sergeant Forbes, Detective Sergeant Baltimore, who was from Antigua, Detective Constable Martin, who was local, and Detective Constable Devonish, who came from Barbados. Detective Sergeant Leston Baltimore, or Sergeant Balti as he was known, would become my closest colleague and a trusted friend.

It was time for me to be educated in the ways of the Caribbean. So I sat back and let my team do the talking. They told me everyone knew who the drug runners were, but that nobody did anything about it. There had only been two significant drug seizures on the islands. The first was of six bales of cannabis found under a local man's bed. He was arrested and taken before the assize court (the criminal court held periodically) where he explained that he had been away for the weekend and, during this time, someone must have put it there. The nine-person jury retired and deliberated for ten minutes before returning their not-guilty verdict. When I asked how that could happen, I was quickly informed that 'he born here'. The jury consisted of his relatives: cousins, husbands and wives of brothers and sisters, even the mother of his child. Lesson number one; introduce vetting for juries.

The second case was equally bizarre. A customs officer had, just by chance in the middle of the night, been parked at the end of the runway at Beef Island Airport with lights on full beam, when in came a light aircraft, which overshot the runway and careered into his car. With both legs broken he was trapped in the car and, when the police arrived, they found the plane was packed with bales of cannabis. The customs officer was dismissed from his job, but never prosecuted. Why? Because 'he born here'.

I learnt that there were two types of people on the islands, those who were born here and those who were not. As a general rule, the locals considered themselves to be above the people from other islands who were referred to dismissively as 'down islanders'. I was to discover racism was certainly not only about the colour of people's skin and it was certainly not peculiar to the BVI. Apparently, this was the way things were on every Caribbean island. If you came from another island and wished to become a citizen of the Virgin Islands, an application would be made and, after a period of anything from seven to ten years, you would be accepted. Your new passport would be stamped with the word 'BELONGER', which was a permanent reminder of your status. You would then be entered on to the voters' register and, among other things, be eligible to sit on a jury. Perhaps a better proportion of belongers on the jury might result in the verdicts reflecting the evidence.

The next couple of weeks were spent touring the islands on the ancient police launch, *Virgin Clipper*, which spent more time being repaired than it did patrolling. There was almost forty miles of open sea between Tortola and the furthest inhabited island, Anegada, and the journey by launch took about six hours. It was far too big an area for police to be patrolling in an ancient launch.

It was important to understand why the BVI had become such a vital area for the drugs trade. It certainly wasn't to supply the locals as their use was minimal and most of the people who did take drugs were using cannabis not cocaine. I doubt if the cocaine use in the BVI would earn a Colombian producer enough money to feed his family for a week. The real advantage of the BVI was the location, which was easily accessible to the US Virgin Islands and Puerto Rico, and, from there, a flight direct to the USA. All the US islands were United States Commonwealth countries, and there was no customs control between them and the United States. It was easy to board a commercial airline in Puerto Rico or St Thomas, with a suitcase of drugs, and walk off in America with almost no chance of being apprehended.

Another reason was that the BVI was about the limit of flying time for a small aircraft leaving Colombia on a tank full of petrol. The general practice was for an aircraft to be loaded with a cargo of cocaine packed into coolers, which were sealed to make them watertight. A two-man crew, consisting of a pilot and a 'kicker', would then fly to a prearranged spot in the Caribbean Sea and literally kick the containers into the sea. Waiting speedboats would retrieve the coolers and transport them to an American island. The aircraft would then land at one of the BVI's airports, refuel and return to Colombia. What could be simpler?

Lastly, as the BVI was so popular with the sailing community, it was easy for any ship loaded with a cargo of drugs, and travelling from Colombia to Europe, to pass unnoticed among the hundreds of pleasure craft sailing in the area.

It wasn't difficult to establish which islanders were transporting drugs. You stand out like a sore thumb if you have no visible means of income, but own a nice house and a speedboat, which only goes out to sea in the evenings and returns the following day with no cargo. It certainly wasn't rocket science to put together a list of probable candidates. The problem was how could we catch them unless they brought the cargo ashore?

There was only one way forward: I needed to build bridges. The problem of drugs transportation was one that affected the US DEA even more than it did my new jurisdiction, but there was no contact between the two sides. It was time to rectify that and arrange a meeting with the DEA in Florida. I knew the correct way of organizing this would be to send an official request, and paperwork would flow from us to them and back again in a time-consuming way with every step documented. Alternatively, I could just jump on a plane to Miami and have a drink with all the friends I had made earlier in my career, when I was chasing the proceeds from the Brink's–Mat robbery.

A couple of days later I was sitting in a Miami bar with half a dozen DEA agents. Like any organization, everybody knows someone somewhere and it didn't take long before I had been introduced, over the phone, to 'Tom', my first contact in Puerto Rico. Next it was time to visit the DEA Intelligence Unit where I found that the DEA had long since given up hope of getting assistance from the BVI police. Asking for help had become a kiss of death to any inquiry. Either there was no response or the suspects were warned. This, together with the fact that any request to enter BVI territory had either been ignored or refused, resulted in no crimes ever being investigated let alone solved. I was determined that things were going to change and I left Miami vowing that the BVI would co-operate fully with the DEA. There was just one proviso: there would be no paperwork and nothing in writing. I didn't want information getting into the wrong hands and suspects being warned that we were on to them. With phase one complete, it was time to meet Tom in Puerto Rico.

The DEA officers were thrilled to think that, at last, they were going to have someone to talk to in the BVI and hopefully information would flow between us. There was, however, still no way they could get permission to set foot on the islands. I decided there had to be a solution and then I realized we just had to play the game a little differently. What if they passed me the information and I made it my own? Why couldn't I produce the information and request the Americans' help? They could then come to the BVI at my request, to assist in any inquiry using their knowledge of known drug dealers. This simple plan was to become invaluable in the next couple of years.

Back in Tortola, the well-worn methods of getting information – work your way up the ladder one step at a time starting with the user and on up through the suppliers until you reach the top – didn't work. It was too close a community and the next supplier up the ladder was likely to be your cousin, your sister's boyfriend or some other relation. You just ran into brick walls. I realized information was going to have to come from ordinary citizens at places that might observe unusual goings-on, such as airports, marinas and landing docks. However, nobody wanted to be seen talking to me. Everyone knew why I was there and I wasn't the most popular person on the islands, as I had been told on many occasions. The criminals I spoke to were quick to inform me that I was doing 'dead man's work' or they'd say, 'We know where you live, we know your wife, we know your car.' Their information pipeline was far superior to mine.

I set up a private phone line so there was no need for people to identify themselves and they could leave an anonymous message. This worked, and the messages left resulted in a number of arrests and the recovery of a limited amount of drugs being removed from the streets. But we knew we weren't setting the world on fire. Fortunately I was due one of my regular strokes of luck and a couple of months later the Royal Navy paid a visit to the BVI. Over drinks onboard their ship we were offered a helicopter tour of the islands; a chance to get up close to places we had never seen before, and my sergeant and I took up the offer. As we climbed above Tortola and reached the highest point of the island, we saw below us a lovely flat piece of cultivated land and, laid out in parallel lines, a field of cannabis plants. I arranged for a team of eight officers to be at the station for 5.00 am the following morning prepared for a hiking expedition.

Arriving at the station I asked if anyone knew how to get to our destination, which was called Upper Huntums Ghut. A uniformed sergeant said he knew it well and that there were three different paths to the top. I told him to take charge, split the troops into three and give them one route each. We set off and, following his instructions, my sergeant and I started a journey to the summit, which was more like rock climbing than hiking. Some four hours later we pulled ourselves over the top of a cliff to be confronted with a sight of all the other officers lying on the ground smiling and drinking water from an old tin bath, which had been used to catch rainwater. They had been there for a couple of hours having taken a leisurely uphill stroll on well-used paths. Collapsing on the ground, I congratulated them on their well-thought out plan to see what the 'honkey' was made of. They burst into laughter, mainly from relief.

We found an old wooden shack in which there were a couple of sets of scales, one cooler containing ready-for-sale packets of cannabis and another cooler with seeds. Photos were taken, including one of the inside wall upon which was written three dates: one six years earlier, one four years and one two. Among the papers strewn about was a photo album with one photo of a local man that an officer identified as Heckel. Surrounding the shack were cannabis plants ranging from young saplings to fully-grown plants almost 5 foot in height. After photographs were taken, the plants were pulled up and taken to the police station.

Officers were sent out to arrest Heckel while we counted the plants. There were just over 4,000, with an estimated street value of well over $50,000. Had the plants all been allowed to grow fully, it could have been four times that. Certainly we had found one of the primary sources for local consumption. It was a good day, not least because it was my birthday, and what a fabulous present.

At first Heckel denied being connected to the plantation, but then we asked him for the dates of birth of his three sons. Of course the dates given matched the dates written on the shack wall, which landed him in it. The following day, officers returned to the plantation to find the shack had been burned to the ground. Eventually Heckel was sentenced to three years' imprisonment. It was my first significant success.

We were on a roll and a couple of weeks later, on a Saturday evening, I was relaxing at home when the phone rang. It was an airport worker that we had been cultivating for a few months. 'Quick,' he said, 'there's a two-seater plane coming in from Colombia and there's a buzz around the place. Something is going down.' I phoned the airport and asked the head immigration officer to make sure that the pilot and passengers were detained and kept under guard. Then I phoned my sergeant. I told him to get our team together and get to the airport pronto. When we arrived, the plane was parked at the edge of the water and, as we approached, we could make out the shape of a man standing on the shoreline. We ran towards him, but he disappeared towards the sea, then there was a roar of an outboard engine and, as we reached the shore, we could just make out the rear of a speedboat as it shot off into the darkness.

We turned our attention to the plane. Opening the cockpit, we found every conceivable space was filled with old American Army kitbags, each one full of yellow, plastic-wrapped packages the size of small bricks. A quick key through the packaging revealed compressed white powder, which was almost certainly very pure cocaine. The amazing part was that the Colombian cartels considered themselves so untouchable that they branded each package with the name of the cartel, in this case 'Medellin'.

The Medellin cartel was formed by the notorious Ochoa Vásquez brothers and Pablo Escobar, and the tentacles of their operation spread throughout South America and the Caribbean into the USA, Canada and Europe. At the height of their power in the 1980s, it was estimated that they were earning about $400,000,000 per week from smuggling cocaine around the world. It was time to talk to our two detained flyers, who were sitting in a room under guard. The problem was they spoke only Spanish.

The guards hadn't searched them and when we emptied their pockets, we found $10,000 in 100-dollar bills. When I asked if they had been watched at all times, I was informed they had been, except when they went to the toilet. I knew then that any contacts or evidence to be gleaned from them had long since been flushed away towards Tortola's sewers. We found an interpreter and started to question the two men. Realizing they had been caught red-handed, they were only too happy to tell their story.

The men had been friends for many years and were both employed as pilots for a well-known Colombian airline. Two days earlier their two families had got together for the evening and, as they were sitting down to dinner, the front door burst open and a number of armed men came in waving their guns. The two pilots had been led away at gunpoint, leaving their families huddled together on the floor with at least three armed men standing over them. They were held in a room overnight and the following day had been taken to a small airport in the country. There, they had watched as the plane was loaded with fourteen heavy army bags, which they knew were filled with cocaine. They were then told to fly the plane to Beef Island Airport in Tortola, park it at the end of the runway as close to the sea as they could get it, leave the plane unlocked and go to a local hotel for the night. The following morning they were to refuel and return home to their families. As a sign of faith, they were handed $10,000 for their co-operation.

I stopped them and asked, 'How many army bags?' to which they replied, 'fourteen.' Swallowing hard I realized that we had only recovered twelve. I asked if they were sure and they said, 'Yes, there were twelve in the plane and one in each side of the nose cone.' More education for me. I thought the doors at the front of the plane were to enable someone to work on the engine; it had never occurred to me that there was storage room in there. We rushed to the airport and recovered two further bags of cocaine. We were now in possession of 500 kilos of what turned out to be 95 per cent pure cocaine.

Cocaine sold on the street averages somewhere between 15 and 20 per cent pure. The original pure cocaine is adulterated by the dealers by adding ingredients such as sugars lactose and mannitol. This bulks up their product to five to seven times its weight, which makes for vast profits.

The cocaine in our charge was worth something in the region of $400 million and was at that time the largest recorded seizure of cocaine by a British police officer.

My relief at recovering the two sacks from the aircraft was palpable. I could just imagine the newspaper headlines if we hadn't. 'Seventy Kilos Of Cocaine Lost By Police', or 'Was It Really Lost Or Is This Police Corruption?' Now it didn't matter. My naivety would go undiscovered and unpunished.

One of the amendments to the drug law on the BVI was that if someone was convicted of possession of more than just a few ounces, they were automatically deemed to be a dealer and were liable to a minimum of five years' imprisonment, which could be imposed by the magistrate. When the pilots were informed of this, they couldn't wait to plead guilty as they realized that a trial by jury at the assize court would result in a much lengthier sentence. But we had major problems. Firstly, we had two police officers in a cell guarding $400 million-worth of cocaine. This was equivalent to the BVI's annual budget for the next twenty years. Secondly, the Colombian drug cartels were renowned for their violence. They do not take kindly to anyone taking their drugs, whether they are law enforcement or not. Finally, there was no way of securing the police station and it was possible to walk straight into the inner sanctum where the cells were located. Two officers with a rifle each was hardly a deterrent to a gang of armed men.

We needed to get rid of the drugs as soon as possible. The governor of the islands made some calls to see if the cocaine could be of any use to the pharmaceutical industry, but was told that it was not pure enough for them to consider purchasing. We had no facility to incinerate it and the fumes would have led to the biggest reggae party in the history of the BVI. We couldn't bury it as the drugs would have been dug up long before we had returned our shovels to the shed. The only possible solution was to throw it in the sea.

Laboratory analysis was carried out and an application was put before the magistrate for disposal, which was granted. The following day we loaded *Virgin Clipper* with the cocaine and, for once, its engines actually burst into life. We invited along a reporter who had been less than supportive about my posting and had written a number of articles implying there was no need for a foreign detective to come to his islands. We wanted him to witness the destruction of the drugs as, at least that way, we could avoid allegations of impropriety at a later stage. Also onboard was the deputy commissioner. There was far too much at stake to take any chances with this operation.

We were well out to sea when the anchor was dropped. We all donned surgical masks to theoretically save ourselves from getting high, and the kitbags were emptied and each packet removed. The packets were cut open to reveal two blocks of cocaine each weighing half a kilo and these were, in turn, passed to me sitting at the back of the boat. Each block was crumbled and dropped into the sea. Fish are obviously not used to a diet of cocaine and we were disturbed to see them float belly up, either comatose or dead. Suddenly, pelicans started swarming above us, tantalized by the offer of a free meal lying on the surface. First one and then hundreds started diving into the waters around the boat, scooping up a beakful and flying away before diving down again for seconds.

It took about four hours to dispose of the cocaine and as I stood, covered in white powder, I realized that, surgical mask or not, my feet were not actually touching the ground. I was (to adopt the Nike catchphrase) walking on air. When I got home, I phoned a doctor friend who brought a bottle of sleeping pills, without which I didn't think I'd have ever slept again. I sat and reflected on an experience that I wasn't in any hurry to repeat.

Within a week we were to discover just how vulnerable we were. I was sitting in my office when Commissioner Thompson rang and asked me to pop down the hall to his office. I walked in to see a man I recognized as a high-ranking officer in the prison service. Thompson asked him to repeat his story and he started to relay the following tale.

He had been sitting at home at about 9.00 pm when there had been a knock on the door. Opening it he was confronted by two well-dressed gentlemen, one white and the other of Puerto Rican appearance. They asked to speak to him on a matter of great importance and so he invited them in. The white man then requested that the officer arrange the escape of the two Colombian pilots presently held in his prison. Without further words, he clicked open his briefcase and spun it round to show the officer the contents; bundle after bundle of 100-dollar bills. He was told that there was $200,000 in untraceable bills, which would be given to him as soon as the men had made good their escape. Petrified, the officer said he'd think of the best way of doing it, and the men shook his hand and told him that he had made a wise decision. He had stayed awake all night before phoning the commissioner and here he was now. We thanked him and told him that there would be no record of him attending the station and, if the men contacted him, he should indicate he was still trying to work out the safest plan for the escape.

Realizing we had very little time, we made some phone calls, and half an hour later we had cells arranged in Wandsworth Prison in London and an agreement that the pilots would serve their prison sentence in Britain. I booked four seats at the back of a British Airways flight from Puerto Rico to London with a promise of two complete rows of seats if the loading on the plane allowed. My friends at the DEA in Puerto

Rico would meet the flight from Tortola, and escort us officers and the prisoners under armed guard to the London plane.

Within five hours of being told of the pending escape attempt, Detective Sergeant Balti and I collected the pilots and boarded an aeroplane at Beef Island Airport. The journey went without a hitch and, after handing the pilots over to the prison officers in London, I had a couple of days to visit my family, and Balti got to see London for the first time. My daughter was delighted to take him on a grand tour of all the sights, which obviously included the changing of the guard. He was quite upset that we hadn't arranged for him to actually meet the Queen.

My squad had a spring in its step. There was a surge of confidence, and the officers became more dedicated and enthusiastic about their duties. The liaison with the DEA was proving profitable, although most of the information was incoming, and resulted in more inquiries for us than for them. Over the next few months we traced a number of fugitives who were wanted for serious offences in America. Some of them had been lying low in the BVI for years. As a result of these arrests I travelled to Miami, Boston, Alabama and other places, giving evidence in their trials.

It was on a trip to Miami that I was to be further educated in the world of drug trafficking. I had arranged to meet some DEA agents for a meal, and I was just leaving the hotel when I received a phone call to say they had been held up and were dealing with a seizure of crack cocaine. This was a relatively new way to take cocaine and something I had never seen. I went down to Dade Police Station where I was shown crack crystals for the first time. I was told the crystals were the result of mixing cocaine with baking soda and cooking it in a microwave to create tiny rocks. The rocks were then smoked in pipes and, because they made a crackling sound when they were heated, this was where the term crack came from. As the fumes were taken straight into the lungs, it offered an instant high, but the high didn't last long and the comedown was very fast. The user now wanted another hit but this was never as good as the first hit and resulted in a never-ending chase for that elusive high. Crack was now the most addictive drug on the streets of America. 'How quickly addictive?' I asked and they pointed to a cell where, sitting on a bench, was a 15-year-old Mexican girl. 'Go and talk to her,' they said and opened the cell door.

She welcomed my company, and was happy to sit and chat. She told me that from the first hit she had to have more, and within days she was running with a gang who would do anything to get the money for their next high. I asked what she had done and she said, 'Robbery, burglary, shoplifting, stealing from home, anything I had to do.' I asked if she'd resorted to selling her body. 'Only twice,' she replied. 'When did you take your first hit?' I asked. With tears running down her cheeks she replied 'Monday'. This was Friday! I left the cell in tears, with a feeling of despair at the total waste of this young life.

It wasn't long before crack came to the islands.

Chapter 15

A Drop in the Ocean

There was a great sense of anticipation towards the end of the year, not for the festivities of Christmas and New Year, but for the impending visit of Princess Diana. She was coming with the two young princes, William and Harry, to spend the festive season on nearby Necker Island, which is owned by Richard Branson. As usual, she was followed by the paparazzi and their telescopic cameras. Every hotel room was taken and everyone who owned a boat of any size had been approached to circle Necker with a cameraman onboard in the hope of getting that one photo of Diana in a bikini, which would sell around the world. There was no doubt that if *Virgin Clipper* could be kept running long enough, she too would be circling the island trying to keep them at bay.

I spent Christmas at home and a few days later, on a Saturday afternoon, my phone rang. Picking it up, I was greeted by the unmistakable American accent of my DEA contact in Puerto Rico. 'Time to go to work,' he said. 'You have an airdrop of cocaine going down at about 5.00 pm tonight. There should be two speedboats waiting at Sandy Cay for a plane from Colombia; usual method, coolers dropped from the plane.' I arranged for my team to meet me and was thrilled to find that *Virgin Clipper* was back in Road Town being refuelled. By 4.00 pm we were bound for Sandy Cay, a small uninhabited island located near to Jost Van Dyke and St John. We'd only been sailing for about half an hour when we spotted a small aircraft circling in the distance; the only problem was it was nowhere near where it should have been. It was circling over the islands of Cooper and Ginger some twelve miles east of its rendezvous point, and in the opposite direction to where we were heading. We turned and passed

Ginger Island, and, as we did so, we were overtaken by two speedboats going flat out towards Virgin Gorda.

Pulling into Spanish Town, Virgin Gorda, we saw the two speedboats were tied up and a group of people were embroiled in a shouting match in Spanish. A very fat man was hurling abuse and gesticulating wildly to his assembled gang. Something had obviously gone wrong, but we could do nothing but watch and wait. We decided to leave and went to the airport, as we were certain the plane had landed. It was now quite dark, and we climbed over the perimeter fence and found the parked plane, then we drove a screwdriver through the plane's tyre and let all the air out of the other. Satisfied that the plane wasn't going anywhere, we returned to town and watched as meetings took place between six Puerto Ricans and three local men, two of whom were brothers from the island. The body language was not friendly.

We were too well known to hang around as then everyone would know we were on their tail, so we boarded *Virgin Clipper* and set off to sea. Once clear of sight, we put out the dinghy and landed quietly back on the island. I needed to get in touch with Puerto Rico to find out if they knew what the hell was going on. I was told that four agents were on their way over and that they were waiting for information from their informant, who was one of the gang. I made arrangements for the agents to be met and taken to my wife Beth who had set up a command centre in the front room of the house we were renting off friends. There was little we could do, but get a couple of hours sleep and wait for the informant to get in touch.

Suddenly, we saw flames leaping into the sky. There had been an enormous explosion on Virgin Gorda. One of the Puerto Ricans had been repairing the fuel line on his speedboat and, not being the brightest man on the planet, had lit a cigarette, causing the fuel to ignite, explode and demolish the speedboat. The man had been thrown into the sea, but had been pulled ashore and was badly burnt. With no medical assistance available on the island, someone had made an emergency call to Puerto Rico, and forty minutes later an air ambulance had arrived and taken the injured man to hospital accompanied by the informant in Puerto Rico. The DEA identified him and put him under close guard. He was well known to them and was wanted for a number of drug offences. If he survived, he was destined for a long prison sentence.

Four agents arrived and, with my wife's help, a command post was set up at our home with a radio control. All we wanted now was information. The informant had been given my phone number, and we needed his call and for him to get back to Virgin Gorda and find out what was happening. A couple of hours later the call came telling us he was on his way back, but before he left he told us the story so far.

The pilot of the plane had got his co-ordinates wrong and, instead of dropping the coolers at Sandy Cay, he had dropped them into the sea just off the uninhabited Ginger Island. The two local brothers who we had seen earlier talking to the Puerto Ricans had watched from Virgin Gorda as the drop was made. Not wanting to miss an opportunity of easy money, they had jumped into their speedboat and rushed out to Ginger Island, managing to recover all the containers. With a boatload of cocaine boasting a street value in excess of $250,000,000, they had gone back to Virgin Gorda and hidden their loot.

The Puerto Ricans had then arrived on the island and demanded their drugs back. The heated discussion we'd stumbled upon had been the brothers demanding a few million dollars and a quantity of cocaine for its return. The meeting had concluded with threats to shoot the brothers and the brothers saying if they did that, they'd never get anything back. They had arranged to meet again the following morning and, hopefully by then, the informant would be back and we would be kept in the picture.

The next day, more threats and counter threats were being thrown from both sides, and by the early evening there had been no agreement. Our situation was hopeless. We had no real evidence, no idea where the drugs were located and all we had was a plane with flat tyres. The day after that was New Year's Eve and at 12.30 am, having heralded in the new year waiting for the phone to ring, we decided to call it a night. I had no sooner got to bed than the call we had been waiting for came. 'It's on the move,' said the informant in a hushed voice. 'Picked up at Beef Island and on the way to St John; three onboard, one local, myself and one Puerto Rican.' All we had to do was intercept it somewhere in St Francis Drake Channel, the stretch of water that separates Tortola from the smaller islands. How difficult could that be?

A quick call to the captain of *Virgin Clipper* and we would be on the move. The phone rang and rang until the sleepy voice of the captain's wife answered and said he was at work. I phoned his girlfriend to be told he was at home. I phoned the mother of a couple of his children who wanted to tell me he was not keeping up his child maintenance payments. We were not only up the creek without a paddle, but without a boat either.

If ever you visit the British Virgin Islands, you must visit Pusser's Store, enjoy a tot of the Royal Navy rum and have a long drink of the famous 'Painkiller' rum cocktail. Consider a second drink, but unless you fancy being flat out on the floor, don't try a third. Pusser's is owned by a wonderful gentleman called Charles 'Chuck' Tobias OBE. A much decorated US marine Pilot, Chuck had made a fortune in electronics, and one day decided to sell his business and sail round the world, accompanied by his two companions, a cheetah and a chimpanzee. After five years, he arrived on the islands, fell in love with them, created a rum company and Pusser's was born.

One day my wife and I were given a ride by Chuck in his sleek new bright-red powerboat. The experience – flying through the air as we went full throttle at 75mph – left us both ashen faced and my wife's hands covered in blisters from gripping the boat's rail. But when he parted company with us, Chuck said, 'Any time you need my help just give me a ring.' This was that time. I picked up the phone and dialled his number.

'Do you know what time it is?' asked Chuck sleepily. 'Yes,' I said over the phone. 'But I need your help. I have to get to St John now.' There was no hesitation and he offered to meet us in ten minutes. Two DEA agents, Sergeant Balti and myself rushed to the moorings, jumped onboard and Chuck opened the throttle. He was in his element; we were terrified. We reached St John just as the drug dealers' boat was reaching the shore and the two men onboard, the informant and one other Puerto Rican, were arrested and detained. There in the boat were six coolers containing 300 kilos of cocaine.

The men were separated and the informant told us that the third man had been dropped off with 4 kilos of cocaine to thank him for his help, and should now be making his way back to Road Town. My wife had been manning the radio all night and a call to her ensured that the police arrived to help the agents with their prisoners. As a new recruit, my wife had passed her first assignment with flying colours. Arriving back at Road Town, I thanked Chuck for his help and he looked at me and said, 'You owe me.' 'Yes I know.' I replied. Chuck looked at me and shaking his head said, 'No, I don't think you do, but I'm going to tell you.' It turns out that six months ago, he had met a wonderful woman and had been taking things slowly. Last night, he cooked her a special dinner – Waldorf salad, Surf and Turf, fillet steak and Lobster Thermidor – and at the end of the meal dropped to one knee and proposed. 'To my delight she accepted,' said Chuck. 'And with a bottle of Champagne in my hand I led her upstairs for the very first time. Then the bloody phone rang. Now you know how much you owe me.'

We caught up with our man and his 4 kilos of cocaine, only to find out that he was a minister of the Emmanuel Baptist Church on Virgin Gorda. He told us he had done it just to get the drugs off the island, although why he was returning with 4 kilos of the stuff he could never quite explain.

The following morning it was back to Virgin Gorda to arrest the three remaining members of the gang. They came easily enough, although the fat man was armed with a revolver, which he made no attempt to use. They were fingerprinted and put in the cells, but there was no point trying to interview them as even if they could speak English, they refused to do so. The fingerprints were sent to Puerto Rico and the following day we learned we were holding two of America's most wanted. The fat man was one of the most violent criminals the agents had ever dealt with, and twice they had attempted, but failed to arrest him after being engaged in a machine-gun shoot out. When the agents found out we weren't armed during the arrest, they told me we were completely mad and, hearing of their past dealings with the gang, I was inclined to agree. Sometimes it's better not to know what you're walking into. I often wonder if the fact that British police officers don't carry guns saved our lives. Perhaps knowing that we were unarmed led them to come with only one revolver between them.

With the men in custody, I was visited by their attorney from Puerto Rico who asked if there was anything that could be done to lighten their sentences or even secure their release on bail. Before I could reply, he asked to use the bathroom and, when he stood up, he spun his opened briefcase towards me. It was packed with bundles of 100-dollar bills. How much I have no idea, but certainly in the hundreds of thousands. On his return I told him how dangerous it was to walk about with that amount of money in his possession and that he should keep the case closed in case someone saw what was inside. He stood up, nodded, thanked me for my time and walked out.

The DEA agents interviewed the men the next day and the prisoners agreed that they would return voluntarily to Puerto Rico to face trial rather than languish in a Tortolan prison far away from their families. The biggest problem now was the lack of evidence against the local Stephens brothers whose boat *Hot Stuff* had been used to transport the cocaine from the plane. It had been confiscated, but I had little reason to hold it much longer. They knew we had nothing on them and denied all knowledge of any wrongdoing. Unless we could get them to America where there was an abundance of evidence, it was unlikely we would get a conviction in the BVI.

In the end, the brothers themselves solved our problem. A couple of days later they demanded the return of their boat so I told them I would see what I could do and asked them to come back the next day. After speaking to my DEA friends, we devised a plan. When the brothers returned, I said that there was bad news and good news. The bad news was that I did not have the authority to return their boat as it had actually been seized by the Americans. The good news was that the Americans were prepared to release it, but they would have to go to Puerto Rico to sign the necessary paperwork. I asked if they would like me to make an appointment for them. I phoned the DEA in their presence and made the appointment for the following day. On arrival in Puerto Rico, they were arrested and threatened with a long sentence in a prison full of Spanish-speaking criminals unless they returned to Road Town and confessed to the part they played in the Virgin Gorda fiasco. They agreed and although they pleaded not guilty, the confessions and the evidence of the DEA informant ensured that they were convicted and sentenced to seven years each. Willis Barry from the Emmanuel Baptist Church, who was caught with the 4 kilos of drugs, was far luckier. Divine intervention had come to his aid and persuaded the jury to find him not guilty.

The amazing part of this story is that all this drama happened under the noses of the world's press who were following Princess Diana. There was cocaine dropping from the sky, boat chases, dead of night explosions, threats of murder and mayhem by America's most wanted, a seizure of drugs valued in excess of $250,000,000, and not one word was ever printed. The best part is they never did get that photo of Princess Diana in a bikini.

Things returned to normal with nothing other than a couple of minor arrests and an abundance of money-laundering investigations, only a few of which were successful. Two wonderful things happened to help us: the first was the arrival of a brand-new motor launch, which Commissioner Ron Thompson had managed to get the British Government to pay for. She was named *Ursula* and was to become a great asset to law enforcement. The second was even more impressive. Although there was no written agreement between the DEA and the BVI, our joint co-operation had been noticed by the powers that be at DEA headquarters. One day Thompson received a phone call from them offering to present us with a fully-restored single-engine aeroplane, which they had seized from drug dealers. This was a fabulous offer, but there was the small matter of running costs. We knew the local government wouldn't pay and so, yet again, Thompson approached the governor. To our amazement and delight, the British Commonwealth Office agreed to fund the plane, provide an RAF pilot and a engineer/navigator for two years. The plane was exclusively for law enforcement, and would be shared between the BVI and the Turks and Caicos Islands, which was another British overseas territory. Now we could move quickly around the islands.

One day, with nothing better to do, my deputy and I were wandering about the islands in a small dinghy with an outboard motor attached, when, just off the southern tip of uninhabited Norman Island (known locally as Treasure Island due to eighteenth-century letters, which describe finding treasure there), we came across a small ship bearing an Argentinian flag. It was anchored, but floating high in the water, so it was obviously not loaded and there were two men on the deck trying very hard not to look at us. We had no markings on the dinghy and didn't want to appear too inquisitive just yet so we travelled to the north side of the island. There, in a sheltered bay, we saw a pile of large sacks as well as two small motorboats and three men attempting to move the sacks behind the bushes at the back of the beach. We sent a message on the radio and *Ursula* was dispatched for her first adventure.

Thirty minutes later we were picked up and continued into the bay. With plenty of officers onboard, it didn't take long to round up three Puerto Ricans and two Colombians. Loading *Ursula* with our haul of contraband took a great deal longer as we recovered 6 tons of cannabis and 20 kilos of cocaine. We headed back to Road Town with the haul and two motorboats in tow, and another man was picked up from the Argentinian-flagged ship, which was chugged back by an officer. We also removed $40,000,000 of drugs from the streets.

The problem, once again, was what to do with the drugs. It was suggested that we burn it in the centre of town and hold a reggae party to end all reggae parties, but once it was weighed, photographed, analyzed and samples were safely stored away, the magistrate gave permission for it to be destroyed. We hired a barge and took the drugs miles out to sea, before opening the sacks and washing the cannabis into the water.

Possession of more than 4 ounces of cannabis automatically results in a sentence of five years and so, when the case came to court, the verdict was a foregone conclusion. Or so we thought. But the magistrate shocked everyone by passing a sentence of three years each. It was inconceivable that he didn't know 6 tons was just a little bit more than 4 ounces.

It was imperative that the sentences were correct for future cases so the attorney general agreed to appeal the sentence and get the correct five years imposed. However, the magistrate was not happy that his decision was being questioned, and gave my officers and me a hard time. Little did I realize just how much he was determined to exact his revenge. Sitting in my office a week later, my office door burst open and one of my squad told me the prisoners had been to court that morning and had been granted leave to appeal their conviction. They had applied for bail, which he had also granted and then he'd released them all. He then rubbed salt into the wounds by sending them down to the social services department with a recommendation that, as they were without funds, they should be given money to enable them to return home. As we hadn't been informed of the prisoners' appearance in court, we'd had no chance to raise an objection. We rushed to the airport in a vain attempt to rearrest for anything that came to mind, but they had gone.

That afternoon I requested to see the magistrate. I entered his office and said, 'Sir, I appreciate it is not my place to question your judgement and I would never seek to do so, but in order to keep the morale of my men as high as possible I need to explain to them why the prisoners were given bail.' He looked me straight in the eye and said, 'You appeal me first, but retribution is mine sayeth the Lord.' I walked out of his office realizing that Caribbean justice sometimes came from a very high place indeed. Even though our appeal was upheld and the judgement stated that the prisoners should be sentenced to five years, this would never be imposed as the birds had long since flown and would not be returning to this nest.

I was coming to the end of my two-year contract and had been offered a one-year extension. Beth and I were undecided. I only had two years until retirement and really didn't know where to spend those last months. A few weeks later the decision was made much easier for us.

My phone rang; it was Gerry, an informant who had given me small pieces of information in the past. He was very excited and wanted to meet in our usual place so, jumping in my car with my trusted Sergeant Balti, off we went to a remote spot on the other side of the island. There, Gerry told us that two men he knew as Willis and Lincoln had 50 kilos of cocaine and wanted to sell it. Gerry had told them that he knew someone who would buy it, but he needed a sample to prove it was OK. Willis had gone away and come back ten minutes later with a bank coin bag containing white powder. Gerry fumbled about in his pocket, pulled out the bag and put it on the table. He had told Willis he needed a couple of days to contact his buyer and they had agreed. 'What do we do now?' he asked. I told him to meet us tomorrow, same time, same place.

Firstly, I needed an official analysis from the crime laboratory in St Thomas and Balti was dispatched to obtain that. Back in the office I phoned the DEA in Puerto Rico and explained the help I needed. They readily agreed for one of their agents to come over and act as the buyer. By the time we met Gerry the following day, we had conformation that the powder was cocaine. It was time to set the trap. Gerry was to arrange a meeting between the two sides in a couple of days' time. His job would be to pick up the two DEA agents at Beef Island Airport and take them to the meeting, which was to take place at a restaurant in a marina called Pusser's Landing. One agent was to act as the buyer and the other as his minder. Balti and I, as well as another agent, would sail into the marina in a hired boat, anchoring in the sea close enough to be able to observe the meeting and record it on film.

Everything was running smoothly, we watched as Willis and Lincoln arrived, and sat themselves at a table furthest away from the bar. We recognized both men; one was in fact the brother of the deputy commissioner of police. This one certainly had to be kept quiet. About thirty minutes later I nearly exploded with mirth as Gerry came walking down the dockside with two DEA agents dressed as archetypal Hollywood criminals. They were both very large black men and the one who was obviously supposed to be the boss was dressed completely in white, including his shoes and wide-brimmed Panama hat. He was dripping in gold from his sunglasses to his neck chain and had rings on every finger. The second was even larger, and was carrying a briefcase and wearing a light coat over his shoulders. Gerry and the pretend buyer sat at the table with Willis and Lincoln, while the pretend minder stood back and surveyed the scene.

The meeting was about ten minutes old when the buyer snapped his fingers, and his minder came to the table and placed the briefcase down. As he did so, he pushed aside his coat to make sure the sellers noticed the revolver tucked into his waistband. The buyer opened the briefcase for a couple of seconds and slammed it closed. Another snap of the fingers and the minder removed the case from the table. We knew the case contained dummy bundles of 100-dollar bills and close inspection could not be allowed. The meeting was over, the men shook hands, and the buyer removed and readjusted his hat before leaving. This was his signal that everything had gone to plan and Gerry drove them straight to the airport where they caught a flight back to Puerto Rico.

A few hours later we met Gerry who told us Willis and Lincoln had been terrified of the two men, and wanted to make sure they didn't upset them in any way. They had agreed to sell them the drugs; it was now just a question of waiting for them to tell Gerry where and when they would make the exchange. Now we had to be reactionary. The criminals were running the show and no plan could be made until we knew the location of the exchange. Luckily the drug dealers knew that the people they were selling to came from Puerto Rico and would need time to travel to the BVI. We prayed that this would give us time to set up the ambush. The old saying 'Prepare for the expected but expect the unexpected' came to mind as we waited for the next move.

Two days later Gerry was contacted and told the exchange would take place the following day. All he knew was that it would be in the middle of the day to give the buyers time to catch the early flight from Puerto

Rico. Gerry was to meet our local dealers at 9.00 am and they would go together to Beef Island Airport to meet the buyers. We had to keep the DEA agents in sight at all times. We watched the morning meeting with Gerry and saw him get in a car with one man driving. A little later we were told by radio that the plane had arrived, and the commentary continued as the agents were met and escorted to the car. Our buyer, who was known as Jerome, was much more conservatively dressed although he kept his hat on. He was, of course, accompanied by his trusted minder carrying the briefcase of money.

The four men got in the car and started their journey while being followed by two of our vehicles. It is almost impossible to follow someone on a tiny island with one main road, but the troops were doing a great job. The police were on the car's tail until it stopped in the car park of a small hotel named *Maria's Inn* where they were met by Willis and Lincoln. The car park was an open space with nowhere to hide and no way of getting close. Unsurprisingly, this is where they chose to do the deal.

Almost instantly, a blue truck with an open back drove into the car park and Jerome approached it, looked into the back and touched his hat, which was the signal that the drugs were there. I ordered everyone to arrest the men, and Sergeant Balti and I ran towards the truck. I was almost at the passenger door when, out of the window, pointing straight at me, was a gun. There was no time to think so instinct took over. I had two choices: to be brave but stupid, grab the gun and get shot, or to be a coward and run like hell, but at least be alive to tell the tale.

As I am writing this book, you will be fully aware of the decision I took. I ran like hell and threw myself into a ditch of stinking water with Balti right beside me. There was chaos in the car park. The truck had made good its escape, throwing up sand and stones from its spinning tyres as it sped away, knocking over Lincoln in the melee. It jumped a ditch and raced away into the town centre, bouncing over pavements as people scampered for safety. One of our officers took up the chase, but was having trouble closing the gap on the flying truck. Lincoln was still lying on the ground in the car park so he was easily arrested, as was

Willis who saw no point in running as he was known to everybody. The good news was that, aside from a few cuts and bruises, nobody had been wounded.

After pulling ourselves out of the smelly ditch with nothing damaged but our pride, one of the officers came over and told us about the two men in the truck. The driver was a man named Philip and the passenger was Dale. Balti looked at me and said, 'You have just had a gun pointed at you by your own deputy's half brother.'

When I arrived home that night, I was in a reflective mood. We had just carried out an operation where one villain was the deputy commissioner's brother and another was my second in command's half-brother. I thought back to my first days in the BVI when I was told that if someone was born here they would have a relative in every local family on the island. Never had anything been so true.

My wife asked what type of gun had been pointed at me and I told her that it appeared to have a hole in the barrel the size of a cannon. It certainly wasn't a starting pistol, but it had achieved the same result. I'm sure if there had been a world record for the 20-yard sprint I would have broken it that morning. Before we fell asleep that night we both knew I would not be signing another year's contract. It was time to go home.

My decision was confirmed when all four men stood before the assize court later that year. Despite the overwhelming evidence of all the officers and the DEA agents, together with photographs, drug samples and the evidence of Gerry the informant, Willis Pickering, Lincoln Frazer, Dale Abramson and Phillip Brewley were found not guilty by the jury. The drugs were never recovered.

My biggest regret was leaving behind the one man to whom I had become very close, Detective Sergeant Baltimore. We would always owe each other so much. There had been times that were good and bad, happy and sad, dangerous and funny. He had become 'our Caribbean son'.

I often ask myself, did we make a difference? Not a big one that's for certain. Perhaps we caused a sting on the skin of the drugs trade; just enough to make them itch for a while. We certainly didn't do enough to slow down the billion-dollar trade, which takes so many young lives. I don't think that will ever happen. The most important thing is that law enforcement must never give up the fight.

We certainly left the British Virgin Islands better equipped to deal with the problems surrounding their shores. The officers were more dedicated and worldlier; they had a new launch and an aircraft to assist with surveillance. Computers had started to arrive (although nobody knew what to do with them). But this is the Caribbean and as soon as the British Government said the BVI had to fund the plane, it was parked at the end of the runway at Beef Island Airport and never flew again. There are at least 5 British Police Officers station there but the priority is now Money Laundering. There is no dedicated Drug Squad. There are at least nine unsolved drug-related murders and yet the actual amount of drugs seized is less than it was twenty-five years ago.

Chapter 16

Back Home

It was time to go to New Scotland Yard to find out where I would be posted for my final eighteen months. I was looking forward to being posted to the drugs squad, where I could pass on contacts and perhaps help a little with my experience. I should have known better. After stupidly suggesting that I might be of value to the drugs intelligence office, I was informed that I'd had enough of a holiday sitting on a beach drinking coconut milk, it was time to get back to the real world. I was to be posted back to Catford and sit behind the same desk I had left two years earlier.

I called in on a friend of mine whose office was one floor down, borrowed his typewriter and typed out my resignation to take effect when I had used up my outstanding leave. I walked out the building with a spring in my step. It was 1990 and I was almost 52-years-old. I had achieved everything I'd hoped for in the police force and I didn't want to spend the rest of my career behind a desk. It was time to try something new. I turned to my second love, which was tennis, and for eighteen years I ran a tennis school coaching talented youngsters. Then someone said I should write a book about my time in the police force. So I did.

The roll call of criminals: where are they now?

Brian 'The Colonel' Robinson.
Has not been seen since his release from prison. According to the rumour mill, he's soaking up the sun somewhere on an island in the Mediterranean.

Micky McAvoy
Last heard of living in Kent with his wife Kathy Meacock and his dogs. I wonder if these dogs are named Brinks and Mat.

Tony White
Although never convicted, he was stripped of his assets and ordered to repay £26 million by the civil courts. He was living on benefits in 1997 when he was arrested and sentenced to twelve years' imprisonment for his part in a £65 million cocaine-smuggling operation.

John Fleming
Never convicted, but came home broke after his proceeds from the robbery were either stolen or taken from him fraudulently by Costa Rican officials, who promised him residence without ever intending that it would be granted.

John 'Little Legs' Lloyd
Although never convicted, he settled with the loss adjusters and repaid some £4 million to stop them seizing everything he owned. In 1995 he was arrested for an £800 million global fraud to steal from cash machines. If successful, it would have undermined the banking system. It was almost certainly conceived by Lloyd and Kenneth Noye. Noye was not prosecuted due to lack of evidence, but Lloyd was sentenced to five years.

Jean Savage
Still living in the same house in West Kingsdown, Kent. She and Lloyd are no longer together.

Michael Relton
Lives quietly in France.

Gordon Parry
With the help of the Panama law firm Mossack Fonseca (later exposed in the Panama Papers), he managed to hide vast sums of money. When

loss adjusters seized his house in Westerham and sold it in auction, the highest bidder was his partner Irene. After his release from prison, Parry returned home to her.

Brian Perry

Having served his time, he returned to running his Peckham minicab firm. On the morning of 16 November 2001, he arrived for work, but as he stepped out of his car, two men approached him, put a gun to his head and shot him dead. No one was convicted.

John Palmer

On 24 June 2015, while on bail for offences in Spain, Palmer was at home in South Weald, Essex, when a man confronted him in his garden and shot him dead. No one was convicted.

Brian Reader

Regained his notoriety in March 2016 when, aged 77, he was sentenced to six years for masterminding the Hatton Garden safety deposit robbery a year earlier. His gang of pensioners had drilled through the vault wall and escaped with millions of pounds' worth of property stolen from the boxes. Reader sat in a wheelchair as the sentence was passed and accepted his fate with a nod. He was an old-time crook who never answered questions when interviewed, never informed and took his punishment without question.

Kenneth Noye

At the time of writing Noye is close to moving to an open prison having served seventeen years of a life sentence for the murder of Stephen Cameron. His first application for parole was refused.

Kieran Kelly

Kelly passed away in Durham's Frankland Prison in 2001. How many murders he committed will never be known, but it was certainly into double figures. Kelly has found himself a place in Irish history as probably the country's most prolific serial killer.

America's Most Wanted

Scott Errico

Still serving two life sentences. Various appeals have failed and he has no release date.

Raymond 'Little Ray' Thompsom

Sentence to life imprisonment for racketeering and drug offences and received a further life term without parole for the murder of James Savoy.

Randy Lanier

Sentenced to life imprisonment without parole. Released in October 2015 after twenty-six years and returned to racing.

Jose Ortiz (the fat man)

Sentenced to twenty-five years' imprisonment in Puerto Rico but escaped.

Carlos Valencia-Lucena (second Puerto Rican criminal)

Sentenced to twenty years' imprisonment in Puerto Rico.

Acknowledgements

Thank you to all my former colleagues, especially Tony and Balti who have helped to fill in the gaps in my diminishing memory. To the people who have listened to my presentations on cruise ships and encouraged me to write a book, thank you. I want to thank Rob and the Dragon Lady for getting me started and to my children Mandy and Ross who always wondered what I really did to put bread on the table. Thanks also to my little brother for his help and supplying all the big words. But my biggest thanks must go to Beth, the wonderful lady who has loved and supported me unconditionally for the last fifty-eight years.